"Voddie Baucham has captured the keys to equipping men to be a leader in their homes. This book provides a practical, biblical view to reform a man's life to reach new heights in leading his home with the future of the kingdom in mind. I highly recommend this book to any man daring enough to step up, press in, and become the shepherd and leader of his home and to help end 'spiritual fatherlessness' in this passivity-saturated nation."

Joe White, Founder, Kanakuk Kamps; author, *FaithTraining*

"Scripture gives us a clear directive to 'look well to the ways of our household.' Unfortunately, for far too many Christian households, that mandate and responsibility gets relegated to anyone or anything but the precious institution known as the family itself. In this powerfully important and timely book, Dr. Baucham challenges the church to reinstate the biblical concept of father-headship of households and to establish and implement the principles of family discipleship. As a wife and mother, I celebrate the clarion call this book offers to those who want to see real revival in the nation by understanding it begins at home."

Janet Parshall, Host and Executive Producer, *In the Market with Janet Parshall*

"In seeking to develop gospel-driven family ministry, there's an unavoidable question that too few resources have clearly answered: How do we develop a church culture that equips and mobilizes men? In *Family Shepherds*, Voddie Baucham goes beyond surface-level solutions that identify biblical masculinity with everything from watching mixed-martial arts to participating in emotionally-charged stadium events. What Voddie provides instead is a simple and straightforward biblical vision for equipping men to embrace their God-ordained roles as servant-leaders. This vision flows from Voddie's commitment to articulate biblically what it means for men to shepherd their families well."

Timothy Paul Jones, Associate Professor of Leadership and Family Ministry Director of the Doctor of Education Program, Southern Baptist Theological Seminary

"Rarely does a church see the husband and father as the key to shepherding his own family. Instead we have developed ministry expertise in the local church that seemingly no longer needs a man to step up and serve as the spiritual leader of his home. There are few mistakes more tragic than this one, and generations have suffered and will suffer if we do not call men to step up and serve as the spiritual leader. *Family Shepherds* is the primary tool that pastors and church leaders need to bridge that gap and to execute the building of the local church as God intended and has communicated in his Word."

Brian Doyle, Founder and President, Iron Sharpens Iron

FAMILY
SHEPHERDS

CALLING AND EQUIPPING MEN
TO LEAD THEIR HOMES

FAMILY
SHEPHERDS

BY THE AUTHOR OF FAMILY DRIVEN FAITH

VODDIE BAUCHAM JR.

CROSSWAY®

WHEATON, ILLINOIS

Library of Congress Cataloging-in-Publication Data

Family shepherds : calling and equipping men to lead their homes / Voddie Baucham, Jr.
    p.   cm.
   Includes bibliographical references.
   ISBN 978-1-4335-2369-4 (tp)
   1. Christian men—Family relationships. 2. Christian men—Religious life. 3. Families—Religious life. I. Title.
BV4528.2.B38   2011
248.8'42—dc23   2011038004

To
the men of GFBC

CONTENTS

INTRODUCTION

REFORMATION BEFORE REVIVAL

Since writing *Family Driven Faith* several years ago, I've had literally hundreds of conversations either in person, on the phone, or via e-mail with pastors, denominational leaders, and fathers of every stripe who echo the same sentiment: we need a revival of family religion!

To which I respond, "Amen"—but also, "Not so fast."

Before we can have a revival, we need a reformation. Just like Luther, Calvin, Zwingli, and others looked at Roman Catholicism and held it up to the light of Scripture in the sixteenth century, we need men today who'll do the same with our current ideas of manhood and the family.

There's a generation of men who sense God's Spirit calling them to something more—but without reformation, they have no idea what that "more" looks like. My goal in this book is to offer what I hope to be helpful, biblical, gospel-centered truths that will prepare us to that end. May God use this to spur on the needed reformation. We must forsake our extrabiblical (and sometimes outright *un*biblical) paradigms in favor of biblical ones.

This book is ultimately about the future. The future of your family and mine depends in large part on what we believe and how we behave in light of the truths contained herein. And I assure you, I mean that literally. It's hard to overestimate the importance of the family in general, and fathers in particular. The family is the cornerstone of society. It has been said that as goes the family, so goes the world. It can also be said that as goes the father, so goes the family.

The role of men in their families is so important that God honored it by conferring upon us his own title, Father. We're the governors and guides of our families, and the way we lead has far-reaching implications.

Over the past several years, I've thought, written, taught, and labored long and hard over the issue of male leadership in the home. I've watched families crumble under the weight of paternal neglect. I've seen young men wander aimlessly, looking for answers their fathers should have given them in both word and deed. And I've grieved with Christian women who've grown weary of begging God to make their husbands the spiritual leaders of their homes.

I've also seen men wake up to the responsibility and privilege of being their family's shepherd. I've watched households transform quickly as fathers take the helm and begin to lead and disciple their wives and children. I've seen marriages healed as husbands begin to take seriously their duty to love their wives as Christ loved the church (Eph. 5:25) and to raise their children in the discipline and instruction of the Lord (Eph. 6:4).

This is the kind of transformation to which I desire to contribute. I want to help men overcome a legacy of passivity, incompetence, and indifference. I want to help shape the thinking of a generation of fathers who embrace their role with a certain amount of fear and trembling while carrying out their tasks with faith and confidence.

In short, I want to answer the question I've received from hundreds, if not thousands, of men: *How do I lead my family?*

This is merely one beggar's effort to tell other beggars where he found bread.

THE IMPACT OF PARADIGM

The church I have the privilege of serving—Grace Family Baptist Church in the area just north of Houston—is not a perfect church by any stretch of the imagination. However, it's a church where men's lives and families have been transformed in recent years. More importantly, it's a church where faithfulness to the Word of God has borne much fruit. This fruit has taken the form of conversions in the lives of those who knew they were lost and of some who were church leaders and thought they were saved. The fruit has been borne as well in marriages healed (often without a single counseling session); in families healed; in families embracing the gift of children after having decided to close the womb; and in a host of other God-sized providences.

Let me say more about our church's paradigm and the ways in which we've worked to bring men along in what is to many a radical approach to family and ministry. In our church, the truths contained in this book are lived out in a very unusual way. We don't have specialized ministries designed to aim targeted discipleship at every age and/or constituency. We don't have youth ministers, children's ministers, singles' ministers, etc. Our focus is on equipping family shepherds and holding them accountable for the work to which God has called them. As a result, we are forced to pay a lot more attention to how we view family discipleship.

Our paradigm will seem foreign to many who read this book. However, I don't want you to get caught up in the paradigm. This book is not about a paradigm; it's about the transcendent truths that govern Christian fatherhood. So as I talk about our church, try to remember that regardless of your setting, you can—and must—pursue a gospel-centered, biblically informed approach to your family. Not being in a church like ours is no excuse. Nor is being in a church like ours a guarantee that these things will happen. We must pursue family shepherding, whatever our church environment.

WHAT DRIVES US

Our goal is the gospel. The approach to family shepherding in this book, and the things we do in our church, are not predicated on statistics about church dropouts (though that is important). Nor is it our belief that all the church's problems stem from a low view of the family (though that issue is significant). What we do, and what I'm writing about here, starts with a belief that the gospel is our only hope. The family is not the gospel; nor is the family as important as the gospel. The family is a delivery mechanism for the gospel.

In Ephesians 5 and 6 the role of fathers loving their wives and discipling their children, the responsibility of wives to submit to their husbands, and the duties of parents to their children are all couched in terms that are unmistakable in their gospel-centeredness. This is all about "Christ and the church" (5:32), as Paul declares. It's about the *gospel*. It's about God's redemptive work that began in the garden with the marriage of the first Adam to his bride, and will end at the wedding of the last Adam, Jesus Christ, to his bride at the consummation of history. Every family between the first one and the last serves to remind us of the impact of the fall and our need for redemption.

In the meantime, God has called fathers to walk patiently, purposefully, and prayerfully as we lead our families toward all that is ours in Christ. It's my hope that this book will serve as a tool to help you do just that. In the end, I want you to see Jesus. I want you to see him in a way that drives you to pursue him personally and to keep him before your wife and children in a way that causes them to seek him as well. In short, I want you to shepherd your family in the direction of the Good Shepherd.

PART ONE

THE NEED TO EQUIP FAMILY SHEPHERDS

GAINING A MORE BIBLICAL VIEW OF THE FAMILY

CHAPTER ONE

THE BIBLE AND THE FAMILY'S ROLE IN DISCIPLESHIP

Ask any Christian, "Who is responsible for discipling children?" and you're likely to get the right answer: "Their parents." However, probe further and you'll find confusion, conflation, equivocation, and perhaps downright indignation toward any approach to discipleship that's actually predicated on this unquestioned premise. While we all agree on the clear biblical mandate for parents to disciple their children, we're unclear as to what that entails. We're even less clear on the role the church is to play in offering instruction and support in this endeavor.

Part of the problem lies in that we usually begin from the wrong starting point. Virtually all the debate over the discipleship of young people begins with the assumption that church structures and programs such as the nursery, children's church, Sunday school, and youth group are foundational discipleship tools, and whatever happens must take place within that framework. But what if those things didn't exist? What if there were no nurseries, or youth groups, or Sunday schools? How, then, would we propose a plan for one generation to "tell to the coming generation the glorious deeds of the LORD, and his might, and the wonders that he has done" (Ps. 78:4)?

Fortunately, we don't have to invent such a scenario from scratch. All we have to do is open the pages of the Bible and begin reading. There we find a world where the aforementioned programs and ministries did not exist; there we find a disciple-making model that looks almost nothing like the institutional structures with which we've become so familiar. And there we find family shepherds.

Charles Hodge was president of Princeton Theological Seminary during its heyday in the mid-nineteenth century. Back then, "Princeton Theology" was the gold standard in Reformed circles. Hodge, and consequently Princeton, was on the cutting edge in the battle against both liberalism and mysticism. This theological giant, like many in his day, also had much to say about the family in general and family religion in particular. "The head of the family," Hodge stated, "should be able to read the Scriptures as well as to lead in the prayer. . . . All persons subject to the watch or care of the Church should be required to maintain in their households this stated worship of God. . . . A man's responsibility to his children, as well as to God, binds him to make his house a Bethel; if not a Bethel, it will be a dwelling place of evil spirits." Hodge also recognized the singular importance of the family in the broader scope of God's redemptive work: "The character of the Church and of the state depends on the character of the family. If religion dies out in the family, it cannot elsewhere be maintained."[1]

Unfortunately, such sentiment has been largely lost. Today it's rare to find such clear, pointed words directed at heads of households concerning their responsibility to shepherd their families. Or, if we do hear them, they're coming from the realm of psychological self-help rather than emanating from the pens of pastors and theologians.

However, things they are a changin'. Little by little, we're beginning to hear the clarion call from voices like R. Albert Mohler, president of Southern Baptist Theological Seminary (the largest seminary in the world) and Wayne Grudem, perhaps the best known theologian of our day, as well as John Piper, the pastor's pastor of the twenty-first century. No longer do we see this issue as one relegated to the limited genre of "family literature"; we're beginning to see this not only as an item of concern, but as one of the most important theological issues of our day.

SACRED COWS VS. SACRIFICIAL LAMBS

The result of the kind of introspection I'm suggesting will be either (1) the destruction of some sacred cows, or (2) the continued slaughter of sacrificial lambs. The sacred cows are numerous (and I intend to identify them both directly and indirectly in the ensuing chapters). Meanwhile the sacrificial lambs represent the myriad families strewn across the battlefields of their broken homes, having been ravaged by passivity, ignorance, cowardice, and usurpation. They're homes with fathers who have no earthly idea how to lead them, let alone the slightest inclination to shoulder the responsibility. What's worse, many of these casualties of war are wearing medals and have trophies on their mantle that read, "For Merely Showing Up"!

The tragedy, of course, is that these same men, had they lived two hundred years ago, would have been reprimanded instead of being rewarded. For example, take the words of the great nineteenth-century English pastor C. H. Spurgeon:

> To neglect the instruction of our offspring is worse than *brutish*. Family religion is *necessary* for the nation, for the family itself, and for the church of God. . . . Would that parents would awaken to a sense of the importance of this matter. It is a pleasant duty to talk of Jesus to our sons and daughters, and the more so because it has often proved to be an *accepted* work, for God has saved the children through the parents' prayers and admonitions. May every house into which this volume shall come honor the Lord and receive his smile.[2]

Far from calling for more, newer, and better youth ministries, Spurgeon, like his contemporaries and his predecessors, understood the crucial and irreplaceable role of the home—and particularly the role of the father as family shepherd—in the day-to-day work of resisting doctrinal error and advancing the gospel.

And before you question whether such an emphasis on fathers and their ministry at home would devalue the work of the pulpit, let me remind you Spurgeon was known as "the Prince of Preachers." No one prior to the modern era, wherein family religion is all but lost, would have offered such an objection. This is not a zero-sum game. We do not rely *either* on the pulpit *or* on the home. Both institutions are charged to play their role in this matter, and neither is called to do so without the other.

But don't take Spurgeon's word for it. Just examine the Scriptures, and you'll find that in both the Old Testament and the New, there is ample evidence to show that he's absolutely right.

THE FAMILY'S ROLE IN THE OLD TESTAMENT

The Old Testament is replete with clear-cut examples of the role of the family in discipling children. However, this is sometimes a hindrance for those who fail to either approach the Scriptures from a more "dispensational" hermeneutic or simply overemphasize the discontinuity between the Old and New Covenants. The result can be a failure to grasp the importance of family discipleship. Nevertheless, an understanding of the Old Testament emphasis on family discipleship is crucial to any real understanding of the concept in the Bible as a whole.

THE DOMINION MANDATE

For God's Old Testament people, "private prayer, morning and evening, hallowed daily life, and family religion pervaded the home."[3] A number of clear passages in the Old Testament point to a father's responsibility to disciple his children (e.g., Deut. 6:6–7; Psalm 78; Proverbs 4), and in other places the implications are so strong as to be unavoidable.

For example, consider God's "dominion mandate" for mankind in Genesis 1:28: "Be fruitful and multiply and fill the earth and subdue it and have dominion over the fish of the sea and over the birds of the heavens and over every living thing that moves on the earth." Jim Hamilton's insights are helpful here: "Adam's job was to rule and subdue the earth. This seems to mean that his task was to expand the borders of Eden until the whole earth was like Eden, a place where God was present, known, served, worshiped, and uniquely present."[4] How can we understand such a mandate apart from a clear call to multigenerational family discipleship?

Of course, Adam failed, and this was followed by God's covenant promise to raise up a "seed" from the woman that would redeem man and defeat Satan (Gen. 3:15). Redemptive history then traces through Israel's history—the patriarchs, Egyptian bondage, deliverance, the Promised Land, exile, and restoration to the land—until at last Israel's national story and her dominion mandate are transformed in the New Testament:

> Eventually God sent Jesus, who recapitulated Israel, withstood temptation, conquered the land, overcame death by dying and rising, and has commissioned his followers to make disciples of all nations. When the full number of the Gentiles has been gathered, Israel will be saved (Romans 11:25–27), and Jesus will cover the dry lands with the glory of Yahweh.[5]

The idea that God's image and glory would be spread abroad throughout the world manifestly implies that one generation will teach the next. So we see in the dominion mandate the absolute necessity of the practice of family discipleship.

PRESERVING THE LAW AND THE COVENANT

Inherent in the dominion mandate is the teaching of the law of God and the perpetuation of the covenant people.

The clearest expression of God's design for teaching his law multigenerationally is seen in the book of Deuteronomy. Here Moses, as he stands on the periphery of the Promised Land, delivers a series of sermons wherein he gives the law again. Moses clearly viewed the multigenerational transmittal of biblical truth as a responsibility shared by the home (Deut. 6:1–15). Clearly the Old Testament offers a mandate to teach God's Law in the context of the home, though it in no way excludes the ministry of God's priests and prophets.

This teaching was designed to do more than just preserve God's people in the Promised Land. God's design was for his people to flourish and grow (Gen. 12:2; 17:4–6; 18:18; 46:3; Deut. 26:5; 32:45–47). We see this not only in the Old Testament portions that set forth the law, but also in the "Writings" or "Wisdom" books as well as the Prophets. The prophet Malachi, for example, declares this about husbands and wives: "Did he not make them one, with a portion of the Spirit in their union? And what was the one God seeking? Godly offspring. So guard yourselves in your spirit, and let none of you be faithless to the wife of your youth" (Mal. 2:15).

Perhaps the most passionate and poetic plea for the perpetuation of God's people is found in these lines from Psalm 78:

> I will utter . . . things that we have heard and known,
>> that our fathers have told us.
> We will not hide them from their children,
>> but tell to the coming generation
> the glorious deeds of the LORD, and his might,
>> and the wonders that he has done.
> He established a testimony in Jacob
>> and appointed a law in Israel,
> which he commanded our fathers
>> to teach to their children,
> that the next generation might know them,
>> the children yet unborn,
> and arise and tell them to their children,
>> so that they should set their hope in God
> and not forget the works of God,
>> but keep his commandments;
> and that they should not be like their fathers,
>> a stubborn and rebellious generation,
> a generation whose heart was not steadfast,
>> whose spirit was not faithful to God. (78:2–8)

Clearly the psalmist understood the importance not only of Israel as a nation, but also individual families within Israel, when it came to maintaining and perpetuating the covenant people.

THE FAMILY'S ROLE IN THE NEW TESTAMENT

One of the recent arguments against churches like ours is that our emphasis lies too much in the Old Testament.[6] In truth, a closer look reveals that (1) there's a vibrant family discipleship ministry in the New Testament, (2) the New Testament acknowledges and affirms the same Old Testament passages which we refer to, and (3) there's nothing in the New Testament to support any approach that would undermine, redefine, or abandon the family discipleship model in the Old Testament

Paul acknowledges Timothy's home discipleship pedigree (2 Tim. 1:4–5; 3:15), insists that a track record of effective discipleship in the home is an important qualification for ministry in the church (1 Tim. 3:4–5), and calls fathers specifically to raise their children in the faith (Eph. 6:4; see also Col. 3:20–21). Alfred Edersheim recognizes this clear pattern among God's people in the New Testament era:

> Although they were undoubtedly . . . without many of the opportunities which we enjoy, there was one sweet practice of family religion, going beyond the prescribed prayers, which enabled them to teach their children from tenderest years to intertwine the Word of God with their daily devotion and daily life.[7]

Admittedly, there aren't many passages in the New Testament devoted to family discipleship. However, one reason for this is that the New Testament writers already assumed the Old Testament in this regard.

The clearest link in the New Testament to the family discipleship pattern of the Old Testament is Ephesians 6:1–4:

> Children, obey your parents in the Lord, for this is right. "Honor your father and mother" (this is the first commandment with a promise), "that it may go well with you and that you may live long in the land." Fathers, do not provoke your children to anger, but bring them up in the discipline and instruction of the Lord.

Here Paul quotes the fifth commandment (Ex. 20:12; Deut. 5:16), then echoes the teaching of Genesis 18:19; Deuteronomy 6:7; 11:19; Psalm 78:4; and Proverbs 22:6 in establishing a pattern of discipleship in the Christian home. Clearly, Paul did not view the Old Testament teaching on family discipleship to be obsolete.

NO NEW PATTERN

While acknowledging these Old Testament precepts, the New Testament makes no effort to introduce a new pattern. As Robert Plummer notes, the New Testament writers "viewed passages in the Old Testament about the importance of parents passing on spiritual truth to their children as authoritative divine instruction. The 'newness' of the new covenant was found in the Messiah's consummated work of salvation and in the regenerative work in the Spirit—not in any radical alterations in parent-child relationships."[8]

While the New Testament does acknowledge the church as a spiritual as opposed to a national people, there's no indication that this distinction overturns the clear pattern of family relationships, responsibility, and discipleship.

As evidence that such a family emphasis is out of place in the new covenant, some have pointed to these words of our Lord: "If anyone comes to me and does not hate his own father and mother and wife and children and brothers and sisters, yes, and even his own life, he cannot be my disciple" (Luke 14:26). However, this statement must be taken in light of the rest of the New Testament.

For example, Paul teaches that families have obligations to one another that must be met (such as taking care of widowed parents, 1 Tim. 5:1–8). It would be disastrous to force a reading of Luke 14:26 that ignores this 1 Timothy passage and others that emphasize that God is indeed "the Father, from whom every family in heaven and on earth is named" (Eph. 3:14–15). In *The Journal of Family Ministry*, Andrew Stirrup comments on this Ephesians 3 passage, showing that abdication of the family's central role in the everyday lives of believers is an untenable position:

> We must take note of the way that the ESV has corrected a misreading of the text. If God is the father of "the whole family" (as the NIV renders this text), the text might indicate that inclusion in the church means that individual family boundaries are lost in the collective, which is the church. It could be taken to imply that our roles and responsibilities within our own families of origin have been abrogated. It might suggest that not only is there no distinction between

Jew and Greek, but also between Stewart and Petrovic, Garcia and Wu, Nguyen and Stephanopoulos. *It would imply that the church is our sole family, the context where fatherly, filial, and fraternal responsibilities should be discharged.*[9]

So there must be balance. Our allegiance is indeed to Christ and his bride, the church. However, our obligations as husbands, wives, mothers, fathers, sons, and daughters are a crucial part of that allegiance. The church/family dynamic is not an either/or scenario. This is a case where we must do both/and.

From Genesis to Revelation, we see a clear picture of the role of the family in redemptive history, and the role of the father in the family. This is no small matter. The Bible leaves no room for fatherhood that doesn't take seriously the responsibility of raising children in the discipline and instruction of the Lord. Whether it's found in the Law, the Prophets, the Gospels, or the Epistles, our calling is clear. *We must shepherd our families.*

CHAPTER TWO

A THREE-PRONGED APPROACH TO BIBLICAL DISCIPLESHIP

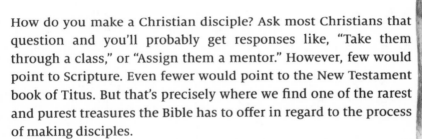

How do you make a Christian disciple? Ask most Christians that question and you'll probably get responses like, "Take them through a class," or "Assign them a mentor." However, few would point to Scripture. Even fewer would point to the New Testament book of Titus. But that's precisely where we find one of the rarest and purest treasures the Bible has to offer in regard to the process of making disciples.

Before we focus on this process, we must understand the purpose behind it. Discipling our children is not about teaching them to behave in a way that won't embarrass us. We're working toward something much more important than that. We're actually raising our children with a view toward leading them to trust and to follow Christ. Moreover, as members of a local body, we're striving to do this work in conjunction with other families who are doing the same. The result is a synergistic thrust designed to propel our children (collectively) into the next generation of kingdom service—and all this is done in utter dependence upon God's grace to do the work. So we must consider the picture Paul paints in Titus from a much broader perspective than that of our own family in isolation; we must view ourselves as part of something vastly greater.

Paul's letter to Titus is marked by an earnest desire to see the gospel proclaimed, preserved, and passed on. As such it contains a succinct yet poignant treatise on discipleship. This is not to say discipleship is the sum total of Paul's message in this letter, but it is a crucial element. For Titus's mission to succeed, he will have to "teach what accords with sound doctrine" (2:1) and "urge the younger men" (2:6); he must "in all respects . . . be a model of good works" (2:7); he must "show integrity, dignity, and sound speech that cannot be condemned, so that an opponent may be put to shame" (2:7–8). He is to "declare these things" and to "exhort and rebuke with all authority" (2:15), and to "remind them" (3:1).

In other words, Titus will have to be a disciple-maker.

Additionally, Paul makes it clear that Titus is not to do this on his own. He charges Titus to appoint elders who "hold firm to the trustworthy word as taught" and who "may be able to give instruction in sound doctrine" (1:9). Titus must urge older women to "teach what is good, and so train the young women" (2:3–4), and he must even call slaves to "adorn the doctrine of God our Savior" (2:10).

An examination of the first two chapters in Titus reveals a pattern I call the "three-legged stool" of discipleship. These three supports are (1) godly, mature men and women in the church; (2) godly, manly pastors and elders; and (3) biblically functioning homes. I like to think of them as three interrelated gifts with which God has blessed his people. This stool is designed to support, constrain, shape, and protect believers (and their children) as they grow to maturity. Each leg in the stool is crucial as they all work synergistically in the discipleship process.

RAISING GODLY, MATURE MEN AND WOMEN

The first leg of the stool is found in the opening paragraph of Titus 2 (a passage which also sheds light on the second leg).[1] Paul writes:

> Older men are to be sober-minded, dignified, self-controlled, sound in faith, in love, and in steadfastness. Older women likewise are to be reverent in behavior, not slanderers or slaves to much wine. (Titus 2:2–3)

With these two simple sentences, Paul introduces us to the importance of *godly, mature men and women* in the church as an important tool in the disciple-making process. Each word in that description is important.

GODLINESS

In Paul's Titus 2 exhortation, the first and most important quality for men and women to possess is godly character. These aren't just older men and women, nor are they simply wise in a worldly sense of the word. These are men and women of spiritual substance.

Many older people in our churches have indeed "changed their ways" for the better. However, not all of them are godly. While some older people no longer live the way they used to because God has transformed their lives—they've undergone the supernatural process of sanctification—others have changed simply because they no longer have the time, energy, or opportunity to pursue the sins they continue to cherish in their hearts. Paul is promoting here the former, not the latter.

MATURITY

Reverence for older men and women was the norm in ancient Near Eastern cultures. As the ancient writer Philo noted, "Among all those nations who have any regard for virtue, the older men are esteemed above the younger."[2] However, when Paul refers to older men and older women, he's speaking not merely of their age, but of the mature character God forges over time as men and women walk with him. This is important, since "the value of their example will depend on their moral character."[3] As Calvin noted in his comments on Titus 2, "Nothing is more shameful than for an old man to indulge in youthful wantonness, and, by his countenance, to strengthen the impudence of the young."[4]

However, moral character is precisely what God works in his people in sanctification. "For those whom he foreknew he also predestined to be conformed to the image of his Son, in order that he might be the firstborn among many brothers" (Rom. 8:29). By God's grace, believers are conformed to the image of Christ. This transformation is not something reserved for super Christians; this is the essence of the Christian life for all. It's what happens as God works in us "both to will and to work for his good pleasure" (Phil. 2:13).

God's plan is that "we all attain to the unity of the faith and of the knowledge of the Son of God, to mature manhood, to the measure of the stature of the fullness of Christ, so that we may no longer be children, tossed to and fro by the waves and carried about by every wind of doctrine, by human cunning, by craftiness in deceitful schemes" (Eph. 4:13–14).

This is the relentless pursuit of the Christian life. "For just as you once presented your members as slaves to impurity and to lawlessness leading to more lawlessness, so now present your members as slaves to righteousness leading to sanctification" (Rom. 6:19). Maturity in Christians is marked not by gray hair, but by the fruit believers bear in keeping with their sanctification. These are the men and women to whom Paul refers in Titus 2.

Godliness and maturity are not only gifts granted by God's Spirit to the individual believer; the context of Titus 2 makes it clear that they're gifts granted to the church for the purpose of discipleship and mentoring. God's design is for godly, mature men and women to impact the lives of younger believers. This is crucial when considering what it takes to equip family shepherds. If we're going to see a generation of young men rise to the occasion and begin to disciple their families, it will be due in large part to the reestablishment of the biblical paradigm of mature believers pouring their lives into younger Christians, and demonstrating godliness and maturity to them by their daily lives.

MEN AND WOMEN

It's important to note that Paul refers to both men and women in Titus 2. While there are instances in Scripture where men and women work together to disciple a man (Acts 18:26), the wisest biblical counsel is for men to disciple men and women to disciple women. Here Paul instructs older women to "train the young women" (Titus 2:4). There's a clear sense of specificity and propriety in his words.

It's the women, not the men, who are charged with giving words of biblical wisdom to younger women, with a view toward encouraging them "to love their husbands and children, to be self-controlled, pure, working at home, kind, and submissive to their own husbands, that the word of God may not be reviled" (Titus 2:4–5). This means that (1) both men and women are necessary in the disciple-making process, (2) there are important boundaries to be observed, and (3) the roles of men and women are distinct.

Thus the work of equipping family shepherds is men's work. However, those family shepherds will have an uphill battle on their hands if younger women do not receive instruction from older women in "loving their husbands and children" and being "submissive to their own husbands."

We must restore order in the home—and this cannot happen apart from the presence and influence of godly, mature men and women in the church.

GODLY, MANLY ELDERS

The second leg of the stool is a bit more elusive than the first, for at least two reasons.

First, it can be difficult to see how having godly, manly elders fits into the family shepherd paradigm. If we're talking about men taking responsibility in their homes, why would it matter what pastors are doing? While the connection may be difficult to grasp at first glance, a closer look will make it clear.

Second, the Titus 2 text itself seems less than straightforward in the way this point is presented. While it's easy to see that God has given elders to serve a disciple-making function, it may be difficult to see how this function goes beyond their pulpit ministry. While it's clear what older women are to be teaching to younger women, it's less clear what older men specifically are to be teaching younger men. It's even less clear what role elders play in this teaching.

A closer look, however, reveals that a list for men correspond-ing to the list for women in Titus 2 is actually found in the first chapter of the epistle, not the second. Of course the list in Titus 1 is of qualifications for elders, but further examination reveals its application to young men as well, for at least three reasons.

First, the list in Titus 1 must also represent the character qualities to be taught to young men simply because of the fact that there's no list for young men anywhere else in the letter.

Second, elders are called to be "examples to the flock" (1 Pet. 5:3). What sense does it make for elders to serve as examples if their list of qualifications is alien to that of ordinary men? What exactly would they be modeling?

Finally, it's clear that the list for qualifications for elders in Titus 1 is also a list of what to teach young men because there's nothing in that list that isn't a proper and legitimate goal for any young man's character. There's nothing there that any of us would not want our own sons to learn and live out.

When we focus on Titus 1, we see that the list of elder qualifications is divided into three categories: (1) the elder's home and family; (2) his personal character; and (3) his teaching ministry. A careful study of these categories reveals not only what elders are called to do, but also what they're called to model, and to whom.

THE ELDER'S HOME AND FAMILY

The first category of elder qualifications focuses on the elder's family life. Paul writes that an elder is to be "above reproach, the husband of one wife, and his children are believers and not open to the charge of debauchery or insubordination" (Titus 1:6). Obviously, this is an area in which all Christian men are called to excel. Moreover, not one of us would be willing to say that marriage and family are areas in which we're willing to compromise in the training of our sons. Hence, elders serve as models for younger men as to what it means to be a husband, father, and manager of a home.

This matter is crucial to our purpose. I believe one of the greatest obstacles to biblical family shepherding is the way we view elders. Today, most churches call men to the office of elder (or pastor or bishop; the terms are used interchangeably in the New Testament) without the slightest examination of their family. I know senior pastors who have been voted into churches before their wives ever entered the door. How could we possibly be serious about elders modeling biblical family life to the benefit of their flock if an evaluation of the elder's home and family is never approached?

And yet, Paul's teaching could not be clearer, and it is reinforced by his other writings. Paul expands on these family-based qualifications in his first letter to Timothy. There he adds that an elder must "manage his own household well, with all dignity keeping his children submissive" (1 Tim. 3:4). He goes on to ask this rhetorical question: "If someone does not know how to manage his own household, how will he care for God's church?" (3:5). Clearly the apostle intended to emphasize the importance of a man's track record as a family shepherd in determining his suitability for leadership in the church.

As long as we don't care whether a man has discipled his wife and children when we're considering him for leadership in the church, we'll never require other men to take seriously their roles as family shepherds. That's why the first part of this reformation must occur in the pulpit.

My prayer is that pastors will take it upon themselves to (1) embrace biblical family religion; (2) instruct their churches as to the importance of the practice; (3) model family shepherding to their flocks; and (4) make a concerted effort to lead the church to examine the home life of all future candidates for leadership.

In the meantime, let us all be about the business of discipling our families regardless of how long it takes to see this kind of revival in church leadership. Who knows? God may raise up new leaders for his church, as men show themselves worthy in their homes.

THE ELDER'S PERSONAL CHARACTER

In addition to an elder's commitment to his family, he must also model general Christian character. Part of Paul's teaching on this is from the perspective of what a godly man is not: "For an overseer, as God's steward, must be above reproach. He must not be arrogant or quick-tempered or a drunkard or violent or greedy for gain" (Titus

1:7). Paul then moves on to the affirmative, and lists what an elder *should* be: "hospitable, a lover of good, self-controlled, upright, holy, and disciplined" (Titus 1:8).

Far from being a list of esoteric requirements attained only by men who take vows of poverty or silence or celibacy, this is the stuff *all* godly Christians are made of. Granted, elders must be exemplary in these areas, but that's due in large part to their mandate to be examples to the flock (1 Pet. 5:3).

THE ELDER'S MINISTRY OF THE WORD

Flowing forth from such godly character is godly instruction. And the instruction an elder must give is related to family shepherding in at least two ways.

First, elders teach the things we all need to know as we shepherd our families. The church is a place of instruction, and those who give the instructions from God's Word play a crucial role in shaping the way we think, believe, and behave in every sphere of our lives, not least in our homes.

Second, elders model sound teaching for the rest of the flock. Men who lead as family shepherds should look to their elders for guidance and instruction on *how* to teach the Word. Unfortunately, this is sometimes a far cry from what we're accustomed to.

I once saw a job posting for a senior pastor on an online career site. I don't remember where the church was, but I do remember two things about it. First, it was a very large church (between five thousand and ten thousand members). I remember this because one of the requirements was that an interested candidate have a track record of growing a church to that size. The other thing I remember is the extremely specific requirements in the area of teaching. They were looking for a candidate who was a strong communicator and proficient in incorporating PowerPoint into his messages. PowerPoint! What a far cry from Paul's exhortation: "He must hold firm to the trustworthy word as taught, so that he may be able to give instruction in sound doctrine and also to rebuke those who contradict it" (Titus 1:9).

BIBLICALLY FUNCTIONING HOMES

The third and final leg of the discipleship stool is the biblically functioning home. We see this directly in Paul's warning in Titus 1:10–11 concerning the urgent need to rebuke those who contradict sound doctrine:

> For there are many who are insubordinate, empty talkers and deceivers, especially those of the circumcision party. They must be silenced, since they are upsetting *whole families* by teaching for shameful gain what they ought not to teach.

The teaching ministry of the elders is therefore linked directly to defending the discipling ministry that's carried out specifically in families. As Calvin notes about these verses:

> If the faith of one individual were in danger of being overturned (for we are speaking of the perdition of a single soul redeemed by the blood of Christ), the pastor should immediately gird himself for the combat; how much less tolerable is it to see whole houses overturned?[5]

All this may sound strange. We're so used to viewing discipleship through the lens of professional, age-segregated, age-appropriate ministry in the church that it's a bit awkward to think about the home being such a central player. However, Paul's words here are not only unambiguous, but also consistent with his teaching elsewhere:

> Children, obey your parents in the Lord, for this is right. "Honor your father and mother" (this is the first commandment with a promise), "that it may go well with you and that you may live long in the land." Fathers, do not provoke your children to anger, but bring them up in the discipline and instruction of the Lord. (Eph. 6:1–4)

We'll look at this passage again, but for now allow me to simply point out the obvious. It is *fathers*—not youth ministers, children's ministers, or preschool ministers (none of which find warrant for their existence in the pages of Scripture)—who are charged with this duty of discipling the next generation. Nor is this—as I've already argued—inconsistent with the centrality of the pulpit ministry of elders in the local church.

In fact, the home is actually the proving ground for elders. As Paul notes in his letter to Timothy:

> He must manage his own household well, with all dignity keeping his children submissive, for if someone does not know how to manage his own household, how will he care for God's church? (1 Tim. 3:4–5)

Hence, it's impossible to overstate the importance of the ministry of the home in the pastoral Epistles. Again and again we find admonitions to parents and children (Eph. 6:4; Col. 3:20) and instructions to elders (1 Tim. 3:4–5; Titus 1:6, 10–12) that center on the disciple-making function of the family, and particularly the family shepherd.

THE LINK THAT JOINS ALL THREE

The importance of family discipleship in the overall ministry of the local church is further evidenced by the way in which the ministry of the home is interwoven into Paul's teaching in Titus. A panoramic view of this short epistle makes it obvious that the home is the hub of Christian activity. Paul emphasizes the importance of the family in evaluating potential elders (1:6–7); as an outpost to be protected doctrinally (1:10–12); as the locus of primary ministry for young women (2:4–5); and as the focus of the instruction of older women to the young.

Therefore, we see that in each of the three prongs of discipleship in the local church—(1) godly, mature men and women; (2) godly, manly elders; and (3) biblically functioning homes—there's a link, in one way or another, to the ministry of the home and the family shepherd. There is thus a synergy between strong Christian homes and strong churches, with the ministry of the family shepherd serving as an indispensable element in the health, well-being, and future of the church.

I've often quoted Richard Baxter on this matter, and his words are so appropriate here that I cannot help but do it again: "The life of religion, and the welfare and glory of both the Church and the State, depend much on family government and duty. If we suffer the neglect of this, we shall undo all."[6]

Amen!

CHAPTER THREE

ONE SHEPHERD'S JOURNEY

Meet the Joneses—a typical churchgoing American family.

Ken and Barbara Jones are longtime members of Third Baptist Church. They've been married fifteen years and have three children. Their daughter Susie is thirteen. She's in seventh grade, active in the church youth ministry, and just starting to spread her wings. Their only son, Billy, is ten. He's not big on church. He is, however, active in Scouts, Little League, and all things PlayStation. Their daughter Amy is seven. At church, she's the apple of the children's director's eye. She absolutely loves going to church, and cannot wait until Vacation Bible School comes back around.

Barbara Jones is a pillar in the church. She's active in Bible Study Fellowship and women's ministry, and has been through Bible studies by Beth Moore, Martha Peace, Kay Arthur, and others. She's a stay-at-home mom with a busy social calendar, but she keeps a journal, does daily devotions, and always has time for her prayer circle. She's the unquestioned spiritual leader of the Jones family.

Ken Jones is a good guy. He's a successful businessman, a devoted husband and father, and a deacon at their church. Ken is not "superspiritual," but he loves the Lord and always makes sure he has his family in church. Last summer he even went on a mission trip to Mexico with the youth ministry and helped put a roof on a church building there.

On the surface, the Joneses are the epitome of the solid Christian family. No one would even think to challenge, let alone question, the Joneses' commitment to the Lord and his church. However, the Joneses are precisely the kind of family that led me to write this book. This is the typical family I've had to counsel numerous times as a pastor.

Barbara is that woman whose constant refrain before the throne of God has been, "Lord, please give my husband a desire and the ability to lead us." She sees the inadequacy and impropriety of her own spiritual leadership in their home. She sees the strain on their marriage and the long-term impact on their children. What she doesn't see is how they got to where they are—or how they can ever escape.

SEPARATION AT HOME

When we look closer at the Jones family, we quickly learn that Ken and Barbara barely know their children. The family's lifestyle is rife with today's typical cultural patterns that separate parents from children both at home and at church. These patterns usually go unnoticed by Christian families until a crisis arises, or until the family is actually forced together.

The Jones family is a sad but all-too-familiar example of the separation that has come to characterize life for the typical American Christian. Mom and Dad each run off to work eight to ten hours a day (often more, when you include drive time), while the children are off at school. Then come their extracurricular activities— sports, Scouts, music and dance lessons, and many more. The parents serve as chauffeurs driving children from activity to activity, but they rarely engage the children spiritually.

At home, they rarely take meals together. And like the typical Christian family of the last century and more, they've never engaged in regular family worship, nor does the idea ever cross their minds.

If you were to walk in on the Joneses during a typical evening, you would find each member of the family in a different room (often in front of a different electronic device), immersed in a different world. Dad's on the couch watching SportsCenter, Mom's getting the children's clothes prepared for the next day, Susie's chatting on Facebook, Billy's playing video games, and young Amy is reading the latest Harry Potter novel on her mother's Kindle.

It's not that the members of this family are engaging in "sinful" activities; the problem's deeper than that. The problem is that this family is in the same house, but they never share the same space. They share an address and a last name, but they don't share *life*.

SEPARATION AT CHURCH

As bad as it is to see the Jones family separated at home, it's even worse to see it at church. One would think that the church would be the one place where a family like the Joneses could actually experience life together, or at least a significant spiritual encounter. But this is rarely the case. In fact, the separation at church is often worse than the separation at home.

As we consider the critical issues related to equipping men to lead in their homes, it's important that we recognize the synergy between what we do as churches and what people do in their families. It's quite unreasonable to assume that things can continue to hinder family discipleship on a corporate level and yet allow us to see success on a personal level. The things we do corporately will go a long way toward determining how much we can expect to change privately. If there's a crisis at church, there will most assuredly be a crisis in the home as well.

I witnessed one such crisis on a ministry trip a while back. My son, Trey, and I flew out west for an event at a Christian college. When we arrived, the campus minister, "Doug," took us to lunch where we got better acquainted, and he brought us up to speed on campus goings-on. During our conversation, Doug confided in us that his family was going through a crisis. Doug had just learned that his daughter, a sixteen-year-old high school student, had not been to church in about a month. I sat there bewildered as I listened to this father explain how such a thing could happen.

As it turns out, it really wasn't that difficult. Doug (like the Joneses) was part of a church that had created two completely separate existences for him and his children. Here's how their normal

Sunday morning schedule scattered everyone in Doug's family at different times:

8:00 a.m.
Doug and his wife are in the "traditional" worship service.
Their daughter is in youth Sunday school.

9:30 a.m.
Doug teaches the college and career Sunday school class.
Doug's wife helps teach children's church.
Their daughter is in the "contemporary" worship service.

11:00 a.m.
Doug and his wife attend adult Sunday school.
Their daughter goes home.

Once Doug's daughter had her license, it became convenient for her to drive herself to and from church. That explains why Doug didn't know his daughter was skipping church until he ran into her Sunday school teacher, who asked if his daughter had been sick for the past several weeks.

Unfortunately, while missing church for a month before your parents know it may be an extreme example, this Sunday morning schedule isn't at all unusual for Christian families attending church today. That's why families like the Joneses don't get relief from their isolation when they go to church—they actually have the isolation reinforced!

But this problem is about more than just everyone being in different buildings.

THIS IS BORING

What families like the Joneses often don't see is their theological and philosophical differences.

Mom and Dad rarely discover this until they're thrust into the same environment. Most Christians think that a service that consists of people in suits, call to worship, hymns, Psalms, readings, prayers, long sermons, and benedictions differ only stylistically from services with people in jeans and graphic T-shirts, opening cover song, welcome, extended contemporary soft-rock praise set, drama, and a brief sermonette. Little do they know that these two expressions of worship are actually expressions of disparate theological convictions.

Sadly, this reality is often passed off as a simple matter of entertainment tastes. Thus, parents will express the difficulty in terms of their children being "bored," as opposed to acknowledging the fact that their children hold to a different philosophy of ministry and have actually (in many cases) never belonged to the same church as their parents. Sure, they went to the same campus, but from the time they were babies, they went their separate ways as soon as they hit the front door.

TAKE ME TO YOUR LEADER

Another major issue behind the need for intentional efforts to equip Ken Jones as a family shepherd is the inevitable conflict arising over the fact that the spiritual leadership of Ken and Barbara in the lives of their children has been usurped. This usurpation has taken place both actively and passively.

The active and more obvious usurpation of spiritual authority happened as a result of a separation similar to what Doug's family experienced in the church. Although the Jones children were never told, "Your parents are no longer the principle spiritual leaders in your life," their thinking was shaped in this direction ever so gradually as they were herded through a system that determined the trajectory of their spiritual development completely independent of their parents' input or knowledge. This wasn't done maliciously; nevertheless, it happened.

The passive and more subtle usurpation of spiritual authority is Mr. Jones's complete absence in the spiritual development of his children. This is what gives the greatest strength to the active usurpation. It was not Mr. Jones, but the children's minister and youth minister who decided what direction his children's discipleship should take. Mr. Jones did not catechize his children, or lead them in family worship, or communicate a clear vision for their spiritual development. What he did communicate to them was this: "The professional ministers at church are your spiritual leaders; they're the ones to whom you must look for vision, direction, and guidance."

Again, none of this was intentional. Mr. Jones was following a ubiquitous pattern. He was doing what every Christian father he knew was doing. Moreover, because he did it with regularity, he was head-and-shoulders above most Christian men. He wasn't out playing golf, tailgating, boating, or otherwise "vegging out" on Sundays like so many nominal Christian men do; Mr. Jones was actually going to church! In his mind, not only was there nothing wrong with what he was doing, but he thought he was absolutely and commendably in the right.

As a result, Mr. Jones has no idea that there's a problem, let alone how to fix it. Were he to walk into a church that promotes a culture of family discipleship (not to mention having the whole family participate together in the same worship service, the same small groups, etc.), he would experience a sort of spiritual whiplash. He would at once be convicted and repulsed by what he encountered. I know, because I've seen it dozens if not hundreds of times.

Here's where the proverbial rubber meets the road. This is where equipping family shepherds comes in.

Once we help Mr. Jones see his proper role and responsibility as a family shepherd, how do we then give him the tools, motivation, confidence, and accountability he needs in order to step into that role and succeed?

What follows is a simple four-part approach designed to show the Mr. Joneses of the world that it *can* be done. Those four parts are (1) family evangelism and discipleship, (2) marriage enrichment, (3) child training, and (4) lifestyle evaluation. Each of these will be addressed in a separate section of this book; for now, let's introduce each one.

FAMILY EVANGELISM AND DISCIPLESHIP

Our goal in the first section of this process is to equip and strengthen men in the basics of family evangelism and discipleship. Stated most simply, we want men to understand the gospel and be able to communicate it at home.

Here we emphasize family worship, catechism, personal evangelism, and apologetics as foundational tools necessary to do the work of making much of Christ at home. We also emphasize the importance of taking the message to our neighbors and extended family through the ministry of hospitality.

MARRIAGE ENRICHMENT

When the Joneses first understand and adopt an emphasis on family discipleship, any weaknesses in their marriage that may have gone unaddressed or unnoticed will likely come to the surface. Men who have neglected their responsibilities as their family's priest, prophet, provider, and protector will often experience pushback from their wives when they suddenly stand up to lead.

It's therefore important that we help men understand what biblical leadership in the home looks like and how to exercise it in a Christ-honoring manner. Every man is a leader in his home and marriage. He may have been a poor leader, but he's a leader nonetheless. As a result, a man who has led his wife poorly will encounter the fruit of that bad leadership when he first makes an effort to lead her well.

CHILD TRAINING

Parents like the Joneses have usually spent very little time with their children. In many cases the children have spent the lion's share of their weekdays in daycare and then school, and a big part of their Sundays in nursery, then children's church, then youth ministry. Therefore many parents simply don't know what their children's spiritual needs are, let alone how to deal with them. Family shepherding thrusts parents into an environment where they're forced to change. The result can be something I call Vacation Syndrome.

Vacation Syndrome is similar to that major meltdown many families experience after the euphoria of the last day of school has worn off. Children who before were gone all day are now in close contact every day with one another and their parents, and eventually sparks will fly. By summer's end they're all at each other's throats, and Mom and Dad can't wait for school to start back again.

But what happens if this change is permanent? What happens when you make a decision that will put you in close contact with no relief in sight? Suddenly those issues that are often swept under the rug have to be dealt with. Parents now actually have to discipline their children; they have to train them.

This section comes with a warning and a promise. The warning: be prepared to see yourself and your children in a whole new (not-so-attractive) light. The promise: it's better to see, know, and address the sin than to pass the buck and fail to engage and disciple your children.

LIFESTYLE EVALUATION

Perhaps the most challenging aspect of our family shepherds overhaul is this last section, where we tackle lifestyle evaluation. Here we'll challenge men to ask hard questions that are rarely asked. Then we do the unthinkable—we take the next step and encourage men to actually answer those tough questions.

They're questions like these: Do you watch too much television? Is your family spread too thin as you run back and forth from soccer to ballet to tennis to piano to whatever else happens to be going on? Is your mortgage too big? Are you carrying too much debt? These questions are rarely asked, let alone answered. However, when men decide that it's time for them to engage in shepherding their families, they often come to a point of crisis where they realize they simply don't have time and resources; adjustments must be made; something has to give. Unfortunately, that something tends to be the spiritual commitment that started the process. Men need help to avoid that all-too-likely scenario.

Lifestyle evaluation is a painful yet necessary process. In fact, you could say that this entire book is one big lifestyle evaluation. If you're a father and family shepherd, you must evaluate your lifestyle in each of these four areas with a view toward bringing your life into conformity with that which God requires of you. Your love for the Lord, your belief in the gospel, and your pity for your family should compel you to take honest inventory and lay yourself bare before the Lord, knowing that he alone can give you what you need to bear fruit in these areas.

If you're a church leader who has picked up this book because you've developed convictions about equipping men to lead in their homes, lifestyle evaluation is required from you as well. You have to ask questions that are not dissimilar to the ones mentioned above. Have you become so committed to pleasing and entertaining people in your ministry that you fear a call to commitment would be off-putting? Are the families in your church spread too thin? Is your church in so much debt that calling families to this kind of commitment gives you pause? Are you leading your own family in a manner that reflects the pattern you wish to set forth for others?

In particular, let's remember this: "None is righteous, no, not one; no one understands; no one seeks for God. All have turned aside; together they have become worthless; no one does good, not even one" (Rom. 3:10–12). Therefore, what lies ahead in this book is a call to repentance and faith. Let us repent of our lack of leadership in our homes, and let us look ahead in faith, believing that God "will restore to you the years that the swarming locust has eaten" (Joel 2:25).

PART TWO

FAMILY DISCIPLESHIP AND EVANGELISM

EQUIPPING MEN TO BE PRIESTS AND PROPHETS IN THEIR HOMES

CHAPTER FOUR

HERALDING THE GOSPEL AT HOME

To the Christian father—the man who longs to be his family's shepherd—John Bunyan wrote these wise words to give a picture of evangelism and discipleship at home:

> First, concerning the spiritual state of his family; he ought to be very diligent and cautious, doing his utmost both to increase faith where it is begun, and to begin it where it is not. Therefore, he must diligently and frequently bring before his family the things of God, from His Holy Word, in accordance with what is suitable for each person. And let no man question his authority from the Word of God for such a practice.

These "things of God" that Bunyan speaks of here are always to be centered on the gospel.

The gospel is the core of the Christian life. The gospel is the message, the hope, and the firm foundation of those who follow Christ. It's the foundation upon which the church is built. It's also the foundation upon which the work of a family shepherd is built. As such, we must be clear on just what we're referring to when we use the word *gospel*.

Most people in our culture believe the gospel is shorthand for the "plan of salvation" or a succinct presentation on how to get saved. Ask the average Christian what the gospel is, and they'll probably respond by reciting a version of the Four Spiritual Laws or the Romans Road. Few will identify the gospel as the good news of God's redemption of fallen man through the person and work of Jesus Christ. However, that's precisely what the gospel is; it's the announcement of good news.

There has been much confusion in recent times about the gospel. Allow me therefore to do two things before defining the gospel in the context of shepherding our families. First, we'll simply take a look at what the gospel is *not*. Afterward we'll examine more closely what the gospel truly *is*. By then we'll have a better grasp on the need and nature of the family shepherd's gospel work in the home.

WHAT THE GOSPEL IS NOT

The first time we took our children to Europe, we saw a living example of culture shock. My son went into the bathroom in the house where we were staying and called out to me in despair. As he pointed to the bidet sitting next to the toilet he asked, "Which one do I use?" After I answered him, he looked back at me quizzically and said, "So what do I do with that one?" I learned a valuable lesson that day: It's sometimes more helpful to know what a thing is *not* than to know what it is.

This is true not just for young boys in European bathrooms, but also for family shepherds attempting to wield the gospel in their homes. With that in mind, allow me to dispel a few myths about the gospel.

THE GOSPEL IS NOT JUST HOW WE GET SAVED

While the gospel is most assuredly the means by which we come to know God, it's not limited to knowing how to get saved. This may seem obvious, but as D. A. Carson has noted:

> For some Christians, "the gospel" is a narrow set of teachings about Jesus and his death and resurrection which, rightly believed, tip people into the kingdom. After that, real discipleship and personal transformation begin, but none of that is integrally related to "the gospel."[1]

Unfortunately, the use of "gospel" tracts, while helpful, has also led to a great deal of confusion. Ask the average Christian what the gospel is, and you are likely to get a *presentation* rather than a definition. The gospel cannot be reduced to the Four Spiritual Laws or the Romans Road. These "gospel presentations" may *contain* the gospel (at least in part), but they are not the gospel.

Viewing the gospel as only the means to salvation amounts to minimizing the gospel and its greater significance—a significance that Tim Keller helpfully clarifies:

> We never "get beyond the gospel" in our Christian life to something more "advanced." The gospel is not the first "step" in a "stairway" of truths, rather, it is more like the "hub" in a "wheel" of truth. The gospel is not just the A-B-C's but the A to Z of Christianity. The gospel is not just the minimum required doctrine necessary to enter the kingdom, but the way we make all progress in the kingdom.[2]

As family shepherds, we must not make the mistake of reducing the gospel to *introductory* status. The gospel is all-encompassing.

THE GOSPEL IS NOT THE TWO GREAT COMMANDMENTS

There's a movement afoot in American evangelicalism that incorporates the great commandments into the summary of the heart of the gospel. The result is the increasingly popular "love God/love people" mantra.

Recently, I did a quick web search to see how many configurations of this phrase I could find on various church websites. The results were astounding. Here are a few examples:

- Love God, Love People
- Love God, Love People, Change the World
- Love God, Love People, Serve the World.
- Love God, Love People, Tell the World
- Love God, Love People, Reach the World!
- Love God, Love People, Serve the World
- Love God, Love People, Serve Both
- Love God, Love People, DO Something about It

There's just one problem. These commandments are indeed central to Christ's life, message, and people (Matt. 22:34–40), "but most emphatically," as D. A. Carson says, "they are not the gospel."[3] In fact, they're the summary of the Law! To love the Lord with all our heart, soul, mind, and strength summarizes the first table of the Law (the first four commandments), while loving our neighbor as ourselves is the sum total of the second table of the Law (commandments five through ten). This, in fact, is Paul's entire point in Romans 13:8–10.

Thus, while many Christians are trying to sidestep the law with the "love God/love people" mantra, they're in fact sidestepping the gospel and running right back to the law.

This is not to say that the commands are bad. Indeed, "The law is holy, and the commandment is holy and righteous and good" (Rom. 7:12). However, the commandment is not the gospel.

WHAT THE GOSPEL IS

What exactly *is* the gospel? Why do we use that word in particular? And why does it matter so much that we get it right?

John Hendryx offers a succinct definition:

> In short, the Gospel is the life-altering news that Jesus Christ, the eternal Son of God, became man, lived a sinless life under the Law, died for sinners, and rose again to reconcile them to himself, eternally victorious over every enemy that stood between God and man.[4]

I'll say more about this later, but for now note that Hendryx doesn't begin with man. Nor does he reduce the matter to sappy sentimentality and a lonely God pining over the prospect of an eternity without *you*. The gospel is not man-centered sentimentality. Michael Horton explains this further:

> It is interesting that the biblical writers chose the word "gospel." The heart of most religions is good advice, good techniques, good programs, good ideas, and good support systems. These drive us deeper into ourselves, to find our inner light, inner goodness, inner voice, or inner resources. Nothing *new* can be found inside us. There is no inner rescuer deep down in my soul; I just hear echoes of my own voice telling me all sorts of crazy things to numb my sense of fear, anxiety, and boredom, the origins of which I cannot truly identify. But the heart of Christianity is Good *News*. It comes not as a task for us to fulfill, a mission for us to accomplish, a game plan for us to follow with the help of life coaches, but as a report that someone

else has already fulfilled, accomplished, followed, and achieved everything for us. Good advice may *help* us in daily direction; the Good News concerning Jesus Christ *saves* us from sin's guilt and tyranny over our lives and the fear of death. It's Good News because it does not depend on us. It is about God and his faithfulness to his own purposes and promises.[5]

The gospel is the glorious, Christ-centered, cross-centered, grace-centered news of what God has done in Jesus Christ (the last Adam) to redeem man from the fall of his federal head (the first Adam) and to give man an eschatological hope that all things will eventually be redeemed in Christ.

THE GOSPEL IS NEWS

The gospel is *news*, first and foremost. The Greek word *evangelion* refers to news, an announcement or message.

Think about it; the gospel is news! Therefore, we don't "live" the gospel; we proclaim it. We can no more live the gospel than live the nightly news. Imagine saying, "Let's go live out last night's eleven o'clock news headline story." That's sheer foolishness. The event has already happened; it cannot be relived. You can live *in light of* the news, or *because of* the news, but you cannot *live the news*. And as famous as certain words of St. Francis of Assisi happen to be, he was wrong; we do not "preach the gospel at all times, and when necessary, use words." Again, imagine the parallel: "Channel 10 News . . . News So Powerful, We Don't Use Words!"

I know this flies in the face of the contemporary vernacular, but this is no minor distinction. This is the difference between a life that views Christ and his finished work as the central message of Christianity and one that views its own experience as the central message. If *Christ's* life is the central message, then I have to tell the news. If *my* life is the central message, then my living is enough.

THE GOSPEL IS GOD-CENTERED

The gospel isn't just any kind of news; the gospel is news from, about, for, and through God.

God, not man, is at the center of the gospel. In fact, the New Testament frequently refers to the gospel as the "gospel of God." Jesus came "proclaiming the gospel of God" (Mark 1:14). Paul was "set apart for the gospel of God" (Rom. 1:1; see also 15:16). He was "ready to share . . . the gospel of God" (1 Thess. 2:8); he "proclaimed . . . the gospel of God" (2:9); and he knew that "the gospel of the glory of the blessed God" had been "entrusted" to him (1 Tim. 1:11). Likewise, Peter warned of what the future held for "those who do not obey the gospel of God" (1 Pet. 4:17).

THE GOSPEL IS CHRIST-CENTERED

"The beginning of the gospel of Jesus Christ, the Son of God"—those are the words Mark chose to begin his Gospel. The message of the New Testament is the message of the "gospel of Christ" (Rom. 15:19; 1 Cor. 9:12; 2 Cor. 2:12; 9:13; 10:14; Gal. 1:7; Phil. 1:27; 1 Thess. 3:2).

Matthew begins his Gospel in this way: "The book of the genealogy of Jesus Christ, the son of David, the son of Abraham" (Matt. 1:1). He thus anchors the person and work of Christ within the first proclamation of the gospel in Genesis 3:15, and points to Jesus as the promised "seed."

John starts his Gospel by going back even further, demonstrating Christ's deity and eternal origins: "In the beginning was the Word, and the Word was with God, and the Word was God. He was in the beginning with God. . . . And the Word became flesh and dwelt among us" (John 1:1–2, 14).

Martin Luther summarized it best: "Gospel is and should be nothing else than a discourse or story about Christ."

THE GOSPEL IS CROSS-CENTERED

The gospel we preach is a bloody gospel. As Don Carson notes, "The gospel is not vaguely theological . . . it is decidedly and concretely Christological, that is, centered on the salvation provided through the vicarious cross-death of the Lord Jesus Christ."[6]

That's why Paul could remind the church at Galatia, "It was before your eyes that Jesus Christ was publicly portrayed as crucified" (Gal. 3:1). And it's why he could say to the church at Corinth,

> Jews demand signs and Greeks seek wisdom, but we preach Christ *crucified*, a stumbling block to Jews and folly to Gentiles, but to those who are called, both Jews and Greeks, Christ the power of God and the wisdom of God. (1 Cor. 1:22–24)

Later in the same letter, Paul adds this:

> And I, when I came to you, brothers, did not come proclaiming to you the testimony of God with lofty speech or wisdom. For I decided to know nothing among you except Jesus Christ and him *crucified*. (1 Cor. 2:1–2)

Indeed, there's no gospel without the cross. The cross is where the message of the gospel is rooted in history and filled with theological significance. There we see an event that occurred in a real place, at a real time, before real witnesses. This event has real consequences as it points to real sin, real pain, real holiness, real righteousness, and real forgiveness.

This historical and theological reality is captured especially well in Peter's words on the day of Pentecost:

> Men of Israel, hear these words: Jesus of Nazareth, a man attested to you by God with mighty works and wonders and signs that God did through him in your midst, as you yourselves know—this Jesus, delivered up according to the definite plan and foreknowledge of God, you crucified and killed by the hands of lawless men. God raised him up, loosing the pangs of death, because it was not possible for him to be held by it. (Acts 2:22–24)

Do you see the history and theology in these words?

This is an important point for the family shepherd. We must not present the gospel to our children as though it were a fairy tale. They must know that these are truths worthy to be believed. These things are verifiable; they really happened. Moreover, because they really happened, their implications are inescapable.

THE GOSPEL IS GRACE-CENTERED

Because the gospel is something *outside* us, it's necessarily grace-centered. The work of the gospel is applied to those who believe—not because of anything in them, but in spite of the fact that there's nothing anyone can do to deserve it. The gospel is good news precisely because it is grace-centered.

What a glorious privilege it is to "testify to the gospel of the grace of God" (Acts 20:24)! There we were, dead in sin and trespasses—when the message of the gospel announced our unmerited deliverance:

> But God, being rich in mercy, because of the great love with which he loved us, even when we were dead in our trespasses, made us alive together with Christ—by grace you have been saved—and raised us up with him and seated us with him in the heavenly places in Christ Jesus, so that in the coming ages he might show the immeasurable riches of his grace in kindness toward us in Christ Jesus. For by grace you have been saved through faith. And this is not your own doing; it is the gift of God, not a result of works, so that no one may boast. (Eph. 2:4–9)

Family shepherds cannot afford to be ignorant concerning these matters. We must know the difference between law and gospel. We must know the difference between committing ourselves to leadership in our families because it's "right," and looking to Christ as the Good Shepherd who, by his grace, will conform us to the will of his Father as we trust and obey him.

We must also know the difference between condemning our family with the law and shepherding them with the gospel. We must know the difference between what the gospel *requires* and what the gospel *produces*.

WHAT THE GOSPEL REQUIRES

All the gospel requires from us is *repentance* and *faith*.

This is the message Jesus conveyed: "From that time Jesus began to preach, saying, 'Repent, for the kingdom of heaven is at hand'" (Matt. 4:17; see also Mark 1:15). This was Peter's message on the day of Pentecost when, filled with the Spirit, he turned to the crowd and said, "Repent and be baptized every one of you in the name of Jesus Christ for the forgiveness of your sins, and you will receive the gift of the Holy Spirit" (Acts 2:38). And again: "Repent therefore, and turn again, that your sins may be blotted out" (Acts 3:19). This is also the message Paul proclaimed at Mars Hill: "The times of ignorance God overlooked, but now he commands all people everywhere to repent" (Acts 17:30).

It's absurd to expect obedience from men who are "dead in the trespasses and sins" (Eph. 2:1)—men who "are in the flesh" and who consequently "cannot please God" (Rom. 8:8). This is the heart of Paul's argument in Galatians. There he makes it clear that we are "justified by faith in Christ and not by works of the law, because by works of the law no one will be justified" (Gal. 2:16). It is not our good works, our righteousness, our obedience that triggers the gospel's effect in our lives; rather, the gospel calls simply for our repentance and our trust in Christ.

This distinction must mark our understanding and proclamation of the gospel.

WHAT THE GOSPEL PRODUCES

While repentance and faith are what the gospel requires, what the gospel produces is obedience to all the Lord's commands.

This is the consistent teaching of the entire New Testament, and nowhere is it clearer than in the epistle of 1 John. John writes:

> Whoever says "I know him" but does not keep his commandments is a liar, and the truth is not in him, but whoever keeps his word, in him truly the love of God is perfected. By this we may know that we are in him: whoever says he abides in him ought to walk in the same way in which he walked. (1 John 2:4–6)

This is in keeping with Paul's comment in 2 Corinthians 5:17 on the nature of true conversion: "Therefore, if anyone is in Christ, he is a new creation. The old has passed away; behold, the new has come." This, of course, is to God's glory, not ours; for it's God who has made us "a chosen race, a royal priesthood, a holy nation, a people for his own possession, that you may proclaim the excellencies of him who called you out of darkness into his marvelous light" (1 Pet. 2:9).

Make no mistake: "It is God who works in you, both to will and to work for his good pleasure" (Phil. 2:13). Our obedience is produced by God, not by us. This obedience is the fruit or evidence of the work of the gospel in our lives. Those who love the Lord keep his commandments (John 14:15, 21). Moreover, Jesus associates the keeping of his commandments with abiding in his love (John 15:10), not trying to earn it.

WHY THESE DISTINCTIONS MATTER

All this may seem like splitting theological hairs, but I assure you these distinctions are crucial. Confusing what the gospel produces with what the gospel requires will lead either to a sterile works-righteousness on the one hand or to lawlessness on the other.

For example, if we work toward getting our unbelieving children to do that which only the gospel can produce in the life of a believer, and fail to point them to the undeniable truth that there's nothing in and of themselves whereby they may obey in a manner that will satisfy God's righteousness, then we're essentially telling them they can please God on their own—something the Bible says is impossible (Rom. 8:8).

On the other hand, if we merely throw up our hands in surrender, never calling our children to repentance and never holding up to them the mirror of God's unattainable standard of righteousness, then our children will think themselves safe and secure when in fact they stand condemned before a holy and righteous judge. They must know that in the Lord's sight, "all our righteous deeds are like a polluted garment" (Isa. 64:6).

Thus, we must teach our children to view the law as "our guardian until Christ came, in order that we might be justified by faith" (Gal. 3:24). Only then does the gospel have its full impact.

THE GOSPEL IS ESCHATOLOGICAL

Finally, it's important to note that the gospel is eschatological—it is our hope not merely in this age, but also in the age to come.

In the here and now, we have hope because we know that, as John Hendryx expresses it, "There is nothing that separates those who believe from their Creator and all the benefits that He promises in him."[7] However, we also have the hope of eternal life. We know that Christ's resurrection *is* our hope, because "he is the beginning, the firstborn from the dead" (Col. 1:18; see also Rev. 1:5); and he is "the firstfruits of those who have fallen asleep" (1 Cor. 15:20).

This has implications for the way we shepherd our families.

First, the eschatological nature of the gospel means we do not view our families as ends in themselves. Family shepherds are not men working to shape perfect families that will meet all their earthly needs. On the contrary, we know that Christ alone can meet our ultimate needs, and that he will fully do so only at the end of this present age. We also know that our family ties are temporal, and it's our ties to the body of Christ that matter eternally. Hence, our greatest desire is to lead our families to the feet of Christ, not to our own.

Second, the eschatological nature of the gospel means we do not hold our wives and children to unreasonable standards. We're all fallen creatures. Perfection is a hope we hold out for the age to come. In the meantime, we enjoy progressive sanctification while we praise God for making us more Christlike from day to day. This means we must not expect from our wives and children that which will be supplied only in the age to come.

Shepherding your family well is a task you must commit to because you know it to be right, and you see it as a means of grace that God will use to bless you and your family. However, it's not a practice that will eliminate all your problems. It is not a cure-all. It's not as though we shepherd our families well for a period of time, then sit back and enjoy the fruit of our labors. Shepherding is an ongoing task. The work isn't done until the Good Shepherd calls us home. In the meantime, we'll have to teach the same lessons over and over, we'll often make the same mistakes again and again, and we must continue to rely on the grace of God to see us through.

We'll have to remind ourselves constantly that the gospel is news to be proclaimed constantly. We'll have to point to the God of the gospel again and again. We'll have to continually remind ourselves and our families of the Christ-centered, cross-centered, grace-centered message. And then one day, "when the chief Shepherd appears" (1 Pet. 5:4), we will see him set all things right.

For now, we do our work and hold out hope—the hope that we find in the gospel.

CHAPTER FIVE

CATECHISM AND CHRISTIAN EDUCATION

"What do you do with a man who's a new believer?"

That's one of the most common questions my church faces when discussing our approach to equipping family shepherds. The common understanding seems to be that children can be discipled only by sophisticated programs led by persons having years of training. However, this is a far cry from the biblical and the historical model.

As we noted earlier, the Bible is void of any pattern or instruction that would clearly point to the establishment of modern age-segregated ministries. Instead, what we see again and again is a pattern characterized by the wisdom of Proverbs: "My son, give me your heart, and let your eyes observe my ways" (Prov. 23:26).

But it's legitimate to ask what this pattern should look like if the family shepherd knows little of God's ways. Enter catechism.

In his memoirs, Jonathan Edwards encouraged heads of households (read: family shepherds) "to revive . . . the ancient good practice of catechizing."[1] This practice, though foreign to many contemporary minds, is an old and trusted family discipleship tool. And while no catechism, creed, or confession is infallible or rises to the level of Scripture, it's important to have tools to define and teach the doctrines we derive from the Bible.

This is especially important since the very benefits catechism provides are needed by a spiritually immature father as well as by his children.

WHAT IS CATECHISM?

Catechism is simply a pedagogical method employing questions and answers to teach a set body of knowledge. It's explained in the following terms by Zacharias Ursinus, the primary author of the Heidelberg Catechism:

> The system of catechizing . . . includes a short, simple, and plain exposition and rehearsal of the Christian doctrine, deduced from the writings of the prophets and apostles, and arranged in the form of questions and answers, adapted to the capacity and comprehension of the ignorant and unlearned; or it is a brief summary of the doctrine of the prophets and apostles, communicated orally to such as are unlearned, which they again are required to repeat.[2]

Ultimately, catechism is a means of teaching Christian doctrine in a concise, repetitive manner. As Martin Luther wrote, "In the catechism, we have a very exact, direct, and short way to the whole Christian religion."

Usually the catechism is derived from a confession of faith. Unfortunately, since there has been a revolt against doctrine in recent years, many churches avoid substantive confessions of faith, and therefore the catechism that is designed to teach them. Consequently, you may have to do some research to discover the catechism that best suits your doctrinal convictions. Not all catechisms are created equal.

WHAT ARE THE BENEFITS OF CATECHISM?

Catechism has many benefits. However, for our purposes here, I'll address just three.

THEOLOGICAL LITERACY

The first and most obvious benefit of catechism is theological literacy. Take, for example, *A Catechism for Boys and Girls*, which we use in our church to teach young children. Here are the first ten questions and answers:

1. Q. *Who made you?*
   A. God made me (Gen. 1:26–27; 2:7; Eccles. 12:1; Acts 17:24–29).
2. Q. *What else did God make?*
   A. God made all things (Genesis 1, especially vv. 1, 31; Acts 14:15; Rom. 11:36; Col. 1:16).
3. Q. *Why did God make you and all things?*
   A. For his own glory (Ps. 19:1; Jer. 9:23–24; Rev. 4:11).
4. Q. *How can you glorify God?*
   A. By loving him and doing what he commands (Eccles. 12:13; Mark 12:29–31; John 15:8–10; 1 Cor. 10:31).
5. Q. *Why ought you to glorify God?*
   A. Because he made me and takes care of me (Rom. 11:36; Rev. 4:11).
6. Q. *Are there more gods than one?*
   A. There is only one God (Deut. 6:4; Jer. 10:10; Mark 12:29; Acts 17:22–31).
7. Q. *In how many persons does this one God exist?*
   A. In three persons (Matt. 3:16–17; John 5:23; 10:30; 14:9–10; 15:26; 16:13–15; 1 John 5:20; 2 John 9; Rev. 1:4–5).
8. Q. *Who are they?*
   A. The Father, the Son, and the Holy Spirit (Matt. 28:19; 2 Cor. 13:14; 1 Pet. 1:2; Jude 20–21).
9. Q. *Who is God?*
   A. God is a Spirit, and does not have a body like men (John 4:24; 2 Cor. 3:17; 1 Tim. 1:17).
10. Q. *Where is God?*
    A. God is everywhere (Ps. 139:7–12; Jer. 23:23–24; Acts 17:27–28).

Keep in mind that these questions are for two-year-olds. This isn't rocket science; these are rudimentary statements. However, they get to the heart of what we believe about the nature of God (the Trinity), the nature of man (a created being), and the purpose of creation (the glory of God), to name just a few.

There are over one hundred questions in this catechism covering the basics of systematic theology. As a result, the catechumen (or pupil)—who will probably take a number of years to remember the entire catechism—will have a firm theological foundation to work from by the time he or she is done. Moreover, the catechist (or instructor)—who will have taught these things hundreds of times by asking the questions, hearing the responses, and correcting wrong answers—will most assuredly have catechized himself in the process.

I cannot think of a more effective tool to put into the hands of a young father (or an older one, for that matter) who's a new convert or has never been discipled. This presents the perfect opportunity for him to grow and learn while beginning to lead his family.

APOLOGETICS TRAINING

In addition to theological literacy, catechism is also beneficial as an apologetics tool.

Apologetics is a discipline rooted in Peter's admonition to be "always . . . prepared to make a defense to anyone who asks you for a reason for the hope that is in you" (1 Pet. 3:15). Thus, apologetics involves (1) fully grasping what you believe (being "always prepared"), (2) knowing why you believe it ("a reason for the hope that is in you"), and (3) being able to communicate this to others effectively ("make a defense").

What better way to prepare a Christian to answer questions about his or her theological beliefs than by teaching those beliefs through a series of questions and answers? Catechism serves thus as a pivotal apologetics tool.

DOCTRINAL UNITY IN THE CHURCH

Catechism has the benefit not only of creating theological literacy and laying the groundwork for effective apologetics, but also of creating doctrinal unity in the church. The all-too-familiar cliché that "doctrine divides" has the dubious honor of being both true and false. It's true in the sense that the greater our emphasis on doctrine, and the clearer we are in communicating our doctrinal distinctions, the more likely we are to see people move away from us as a result.

However, the statement "doctrine divides" is patently false

in that this very process of repelling those who "will not endure sound teaching, but having itching ears they will accumulate for themselves teachers to suit their own passions, and will turn away from listening to the truth and wander off into myths" (2 Tim. 4:3–4) is actually a means of unifying the true church around sound doctrine. It's more accurate to say that "doctrine unites" the true church.

But how do we define and disseminate that doctrine? Can it all be cast upon the pulpit ministry? Absolutely not! While it's important for the pulpit to instruct the flock (Titus 1:9), this instruction must be undergirded by more consistent day-to-day teaching.

In his book *The Reformed Pastor*, Richard Baxter has presented what many view as the seminal work on the role of catechism in the local church. Concerning the role of the home in the process, he writes:

> We must have a special eye upon families, to see that they are well ordered, and the duties of each relation performed. The life of religion, and the welfare and glory of both the Church and the State, depend much on family government and duty. If we suffer the neglect of this, we shall undo all. . . . If any good be begun by the ministry in any soul, a careless, prayerless, worldly family is like to stifle it, or very much hinder it; whereas, if you could but get the rulers of families to do their duty, to take up the work where you left it, and help it on, what abundance of good might be done! I beseech you, therefore, if you desire the reformation and welfare of your people, do all you can to promote family religion.[3]

For Baxter, this important work in the home happens in part as we "persuade the master of every family to cause his children and servants to repeat the Catechism to him."[4] Again, this does not negate the importance of pulpit ministry. On the contrary, the ministry of the home is viewed as an extension of this all-important task. The diligent father isn't working to replace the pastor; he's merely striving to help his family see the importance and relevance of the Word of God that is preached.

SO WHY DON'T WE CATECHIZE ANYMORE?

As I talk to people about the importance and great benefits of catechism, they often seem baffled as to why such an important tool would be forsaken on such a large scale. Why did catechism fall out of favor? Why haven't most families taken up the practice again? Why don't we hear about it from the pulpit or in most seminaries?

While it's beyond the scope of this chapter to explore the rise and fall of catechism, I'll offer a few observations.

PROFESSIONALISM

The world of Christianity has changed dramatically over the centuries. One of the changes that has especially affected family religion—and catechism in particular—is the rise of professionalism. Far from the age when the pastor labored alone in a rural church where he served as preacher, worship leader, Bible study leader, and counselor, today we have niche professionals for everything. So prevalent is this phenomenon that John Piper devoted an entire book to it, which he entitled *Brothers, We Are Not Professionals*.

As a result of this growing professionalism, there's a general idea that anything that needs to be done for the advance of the mission of the church has to be done by a paid specialist. The consequences of this attitude are myriad. And there's perhaps no area of the Christian life that has been affected more negatively than the ministry of the home.

As the number of paid religious professionals has risen in recent decades, there has been a corresponding decline in the urgency and consistency with which parents—and particularly fathers—have viewed themselves as the principle disciplers of their children. And why shouldn't this be the case? If the church hires a youth pastor, a senior high pastor, a middle school pastor, associates for high school and middle school (separate ones for boys and for girls), a children's pastor, and a preschool director—many of whom have specialized degrees in their field from reputable seminaries—then why should a father who has no titles, positions, or special training dare to take it upon himself to do what these men and women have spent years preparing for? Isn't letting go of the reins and allowing the "professionals" to do their job the wise thing to do?

Of course, setting fathers aside is never the intent of this build-up in professional staff. Even a church with a half-dozen full-time staff working with children and youth (something that's more common than you might expect) will profess to exist in "support" of families. Read the websites—these churches all claim to believe that "parents are the 'primary' disciplers" of children, and that the professionals exist only to "come alongside" mom and dad. However, a quick glance at the schedules, curricula, and structures reveals the truth. They're providing the whole enchilada, and any family committed to participating fully will have little time to implement what I'm advocating here.

This is not to say there's no room for multiple-staff ministries. However, we're naive if we think the exponential growth in the number of "professionals" on staff at our churches hasn't had a deleterious effect on the average Christian's view of himself in the grand scheme of things. If you don't believe me, try to picture what your spiritual life would be like if you didn't have all the "professionals."

It's like going to a store that doesn't have workers to bag your groceries, when that's all you're used to. Your first thought is, "This is strange." As you resign yourself to bagging your own things, you quickly realize that you don't know what you're doing. Finally, you begin to do the cost/benefit analysis in your head and decide that it's not worth the savings. The next time you shop, you go where the professional help is.

We've seen this same phenomenon at our church. People show up wondering where all the professionals are, then have to decide whether they really want to do the job they've been assigned. Unfortunately, some are out the door before we can even help them with the cost/benefit analysis.

DECISIONISM

Another reason we don't catechize anymore has to do with our understanding of salvation. "I want my children to know and trust

Christ. I don't want them to learn by cold, rote memorization." So goes the familiar refrain. We view salvation through the lens of our modern culture that is predominantly Semi-Pelagian (more on that later). Just think about the phrases we use to describe the salvation experience: "I gave my life to Christ"; "I made a decision for Christ"; "I invited Jesus into my heart." These phrases are so familiar that you probably feel uncomfortable reading any criticism of them.

However, notice how man-centered, experiential, and unbiblical these phrases are. What of repentance? What of believing the gospel? When we believe salvation is all about man exercising his will in making the right decision, our methods of evangelism tend to be emotional and manipulative ("Jesus went all the way to the cross for you; surely you can come down the aisle for him"). On the other hand, if we really believe that the gospel "is the power of God for salvation" (Rom. 1:16)—rather than salvation coming through the power of our skill or persuasiveness, or the exercise of a fallen sinner's corrupt will—then our goal is to be as clear as possible in presenting the message of God's redemptive work in Christ.

Many a pastor could testify to the anguish experienced by men and women who were manipulated into a "decision" at a young age only to realize later that they never understood the gospel, and therefore saw no fruit whatsoever as a result of their "decision." The result is often a recurring cycle of doubt, recommitment, rededication, then more doubt. What should a pastor worth his salt do with those in such despair? He must go back and lay out the basic truths of the gospel for these poor tormented souls, encouraging them to trust in Christ and what he has accomplished as opposed to the sincerity or accuracy of their decision.

And notice the starting point—we're to go back to those "basic truths." Which basic truths? The same ones we find in a good catechism.

SLOTH

You can be in a church with clear boundaries concerning the family and its responsibility in multigenerational discipleship, a clear understanding of the gospel, and a commitment to a catechetical approach—yet still find families that don't catechize due to the most powerful foe of them all. I'm speaking of *sloth*. When the rubber meets the road, we're just plain lazy!

This is not a new phenomenon. No doubt, Christians have struggled to find the time and energy to catechize since the advent of catechism. However, I assure you it's worth the effort. There's indeed a great reward that awaits those who will persevere in this matter.

The great Princeton theologian of a century ago, B. B. Warfield, addressed the same issue in his day. As his words are quite fitting, I'll end this chapter with them:

> No doubt it requires some effort whether to teach or to learn the Shorter Catechism. It requires some effort whether to teach or to learn the grounds of any department of knowledge. Our children— some of them at least—groan over even primary arithmetic, and find sentence-analysis a burden. Even the conquest of the art of reading has proved such a task that "reading without tears" is deemed an achievement. We think, nevertheless, that the acquisition of arithmetic, grammar, and reading is worth the pains it costs the teacher to teach, and the pain it costs the learner to learn them. Do we not think the acquisition of the grounds of religion worth some effort, and even, if need be, some tears?[5]

CHAPTER SIX

FAMILY WORSHIP

Though family worship has fallen out of favor, the essential nature of the practice was recognized and esteemed throughout the history of the church. For example, both the Westminster and the Second London Baptist confessions contain the identical phrase, "God is to be worshiped everywhere in spirit and in truth; as in private families daily, and in secret each one by himself." J. M. Pendleton's ubiquitous (or infamous, depending on your perspective) Baptist Church Covenant has been used for over a century to commit new church members to, among other things, "family and secret devotions."

I've written much on family worship.[1] I don't intend to rehash it all in this chapter. However, it's impossible to talk about equipping family shepherds without addressing the issue of family worship. Regular family worship may well have greater impact on the spiritual life of a man's family than any other practice he commits himself to.

WHITEFIELD'S FIVE ARGUMENTS

One of the most persuasive arguments for family worship I've ever encountered is that of George Whitefield in his sermon "The Great Duty of Family Religion." I think all family shepherds do well to examine themselves in light of his counsel.

In this sermon, Whitefield offers five arguments in favor of this crucial practice.

GRATITUDE TO GOD

Whitefield's first argument is that we ought to engage in regular family worship out of gratitude to God:

> Your lot, every one must confess, is cast in a fair ground: provi-
> dence hath given you a goodly heritage, above many of your fellow-
> creatures, and therefore, out of a principle of gratitude, you ought
> to endeavor, as much as in you lies, to make every person of your
> respective households to call upon him as long as they live: not to
> mention that the authority with which God has invested you, as par-
> ents and governors of families, is a talent committed to your trust,
> and which you are bound to improve to your Master's honor.[2]

God has indeed been good to us. As a reader of this book,
consider your own situation. If you're like most men I know, you
didn't grow up seeing these concepts lived out; your father didn't
lead your family in regular family devotions. However, here you
are, by the grace of God, considering these very things as a means
of blessing, growing, nurturing, and ministering to your family.
And if you did grow up in one of those rare households in the past
two hundred years that practiced family worship, how much more
should you exalt the Lord for the wonderful gift and heritage he
has given you.

For those of us who wish we'd had such a godly heritage, it
would be hypocritical to deprive our children of that which we
long for when it's in our power to give it to them. And it would be
even more so for those who were blessed by the practice.

Family shepherds ought to be motivated out of gratitude for
God's goodness to bring their families before the Lord in regular
family worship.

LOVE AND PITY FOR YOUR CHILDREN

Whitefield's second argument is that we ought to engage in regular
family worship out of love and pity for our children. While this
may seem obvious, let's not forget that this practice has all but dis-
appeared in modern American Christian culture. Whitefield could
easily have been preaching in the streets of modern-day America
when he thundered:

> It is true indeed, parents seldom forget to provide for their children's
> bodies (though, it is to be feared, some men are so far sunk beneath

the beasts that perish as to neglect even that), but then how often do they forget, or rather, when do they remember, to secure the salvation of their immortal souls?[3]

I've often said that our idea of successful parenting can be summed up as follows: We desire to give our children more than our parents gave us, and then to see that they're sufficiently educated so they can give their own children even more. There's little desire for, or cognizance of, spiritual legacy. Parenting, especially when it comes to fathers, has been reduced to a materialistic endeavor. A man with a job that takes him away from his wife and children and removes all possibility of spiritual influence now takes solace in the fact that he's "working to give them what really matters."

However, if we truly believe Jesus when he affirms, "Man shall not live by bread alone, but by every word that comes from the mouth of God" (Matt. 4:4), and, "Seek first the kingdom of God and his righteousness, and all these things will be added to you" (Matt. 6:33), then how do we *not* change our priorities? How do our hearts not burn with a desire to bring God's Word before our families as often as we might in an effort to see the souls of our children converted? How do we keep the tears from flowing as we consider even the possibility that one of these precious ones may not spend eternity with us in the presence of him who's our all in all? And how do we not tremble at the prospect of our neglect being a contributing factor in such a tragedy?

Indeed, love and pity for our children ought to motivate us to engage in regular family worship.

COMMON HONESTY AND JUSTICE

Whitefield's third argument is that we ought to engage in regular family worship out of a sense of common honesty and justice. Here he makes a more subtle, yet poignant, observation:

This is a principle which all men would be thought to act upon. But certainly, if any may be truly censured for their injustice, none can

> be more liable to such censure than those who think themselves in-
> jured if their servants withdraw themselves from their bodily work,
> and yet they in return take no care of their inestimable souls. For is
> it just that servants should spend their time and strength in their
> master's service, and masters not at the same time give them what is
> just and equal for their service?[4]

Family shepherds must see the spiritual leadership of their families as their God-given duty. This is not a program! This is the responsibility God has laid at the doorstep of every man who carries the title *father*. Those who neglect the spiritual welfare of their families are therefore derelict in their duties in the same way a hired hand would be if he were caught sleeping on the job.

This is far from a guilt trip; this is a warning. For too long heads of household have been led to believe that bringing their children to church and dropping them off to be discipled by the profession- als is the extent of their parental duties when it comes to their chil- dren's spiritual development. That's why spiritual passivity has be- come such an epidemic. Unfortunately, the result is a generation of workers who, unless the Lord tarries, will be caught lying down on the job when their master returns.

SELF-INTEREST

Whitefield's fourth argument, and perhaps his most honest, is that we ought to engage in regular family worship out of self-interest. Though false piety often prevents us from acknowledging it, God has promised much to those who love, fear, and serve him. And though God, and not what he gives, is our great goal, it's important to acknowledge that he blesses those who obey him:

> This weighs greatly with you in other matters: be then persuaded to
> let it have a due and full influence on you in this: and if it has, if
> you have but faith as a grain of mustard-seed, how can you avoid
> believing that promoting family-religion will be the best means to
> promote your own temporal, as well as eternal welfare? For "Godli-
> ness has the promise of the life that now is, as well as that which is
> to come."[5]

The nineteenth-century American pastor James W. Alexander provided several fundamental reasons for family worship in his classic work *Thoughts on Family Worship*. In this summary of a portion of that work, we see the many blessings attached to regular family worship:[6]

> Nothing will spur a father toward godly, spiritual discipline in his own walk with Christ more than leading his family in worship. In order to teach his wife and children, he will have to study the Scriptures on his own. A godly woman will be encouraged and inspired as she sees her husband take responsibility and lead in family worship. This practice sets a tone of harmony and love in the household and is a source of strength when they go through affliction together. As they pray for each other their mutual love is strengthened. Reading and memorizing Scripture and the catechisms of the church results in incredible development of children, both spiritually and intellectually. What families regard as important is evidenced by the manner in which they spend their time. Therefore, regular family worship shows the children that their parents believe that Jesus Christ is central to all of life. This practice leaves a legacy that will benefit thousands in generations to come.[7]

Thus, there are great blessings for fathers and mothers, for marriages, for children, and for families as a whole in the practice of regular family worship. Though this may not be our goal, it's a valid by-product, and not one to be ignored.

THE TERRORS OF THE LORD

Whitefield's final argument is that we ought to engage in regular family worship out of fear of what he calls the terrors of the Lord. Here I dare not let my words interfere with the expressions of one who lived in days when men rightly thought much of the terrors to come:

> Remember, the time will come, and that perhaps very shortly, when we must all appear before the judgment-seat of Christ; where we must give a solemn and strict account how we have had our conversation, in our respective families in this world. How will you endure to see your children and servants (who ought to be your joy and

crown of rejoicing in the day of our Lord Jesus Christ) coming out as so many swift witnesses against you; cursing the father that begot them, the womb that bare them, the paps which they have sucked, and the day they ever entered into your houses? Think you not the damnation which men must endure for their own sins will be sufficient, that they need load themselves with the additional guilt of being accessory to the damnation of others also? O consider this, all ye that forget to serve the Lord with your respective households, "lest he pluck you away, and there be none to deliver you!"[8]

An unpleasant thought, to say the least! However, it's a thought rooted in scriptural warnings: "If I say to the wicked, O wicked one, you shall surely die, and you do not speak to warn the wicked to turn from his way, that wicked person shall die in his iniquity, but his blood I will require at your hand" (Ezek. 33:8; see also 3:18).

The idea is not that God sits idly by twiddling his thumbs while we figure out whether we're going to exert ourselves so that our children may be saved. Both Alexander and Whitefield believed in the sovereignty of God in the salvation of sinners. However, they also believed in a God who is sovereign over the means as well as the ends of salvation.

The twentieth-century American theologian Loraine Boettner, in his classic work *The Reformed Doctrine of Predestination*, answers this common objection:

> The objection that the doctrine of Predestination discourages all motives to exertion, is based on the fallacy that the ends are determined without reference to the means. It is not merely a few isolated events here and there that have been foreordained, but the whole chain of events, with all of their inter-relations and connections. All of parts form a unit in the Divine plan. If the means should fail, so would the ends. If God has purposed that a man shall reap, He has also purposed that he shall sow. If God has ordained a man to be saved, He has also ordained that he shall hear the Gospel, and that he shall believe and repent. . . . If we engage in the Lord's service and make diligent use of the means which He has prescribed, we have the great encouragement of knowing that it is by these very means that He has determined to accomplish His great work.[9]

What does this say about a man who believes that God saves sinners by means of the preaching of the gospel, yet he will not proclaim it? Can a man who's truly converted neglect to share the good news with his own children as early and as often as possible? Certainly not! Family shepherds must be reminded of this great duty, and of the accountability by which it's accompanied.

FAMILY WORSHIP IN SIMPLE PRACTICE

Now that we know *why* we should have family worship, the next question ought to be, "What does it look like?"

Family worship isn't a full-on church service every day; instead it's a brief time of devotion before the Lord. The elements are singing, Scripture reading, and prayer. That's it! You sing together, pray together, and read the Scriptures together. Giving fifteen to twenty minutes a day to these simple practices will transform your family.

What do we sing? You can sing the great hymns of the faith, Scripture memory songs, family favorites, or other songs that you normally use in church. The goal is to help your children learn great truths through music. If you have younger children, you may want to stay with one song for a week or even a month, so they learn through the repetition.

What do we read? You can read a daily chapter from the book of Proverbs. Since Proverbs has thirty-one chapters, in most months you can read through the entire book, always reading the chapter that corresponds to the day of the month. You can also pick a book of the Bible and work your way through it a paragraph at a time or even a chapter at a time. We've also seen great benefit in reading through our church's confession of faith.

How do we pray? This is often the most difficult aspect of family worship. Most families aren't in the habit of praying aloud together, and frankly, most of us just aren't comfortable doing so. However, we must. Try praying for one another. Write down prayer requests for the week and pray through them, tracking the ways in which God answers. Pray for those in governmental authority (1 Timothy 2); obtain a list of local, state, and national leaders and intercede for each of them. Pray that the Lord of the harvest will send forth laborers (Matt. 9:38). Pray for people who have yet to hear the gospel. Pray for those who lead your church. Make a list of these categories and you'll be well on your way to establishing a vital prayer ministry in your home.

When do we do it? Find a time that works for your family. Do all of you wake up early in the morning? Do it then. Do you eat breakfast, lunch, or dinner together? That will work too. Do you have time in the evening before bed? Why not then? Find a time that will allow you to be consistent and stick to it.

But the bottom line is—just do it! This is important stuff.

Finally, let the words of that great evangelist George Whitefield warm your heart to this inestimably important task:

> That there may be always such a heart in you, let me exhort all governors of families, in the name of our Lord Jesus Christ, often to reflect on the inestimable worth of their own souls, and the infinite ransom, even the precious blood of Jesus Christ, which has been paid down for them.
>
> Remember, I beseech you to remember, that you are fallen creatures; that you are by nature lost and estranged from God; and that you can never be restored to your primitive happiness, till by being born again of the Holy Ghost, you arrive at your primitive state of purity, have the image of God re-stamped upon your souls, and are thereby made meet to be partakers of the inheritance with the saints in light.
>
> Do, I say, but seriously and frequently reflect on, and act as persons that believe such important truths, and you will no more neglect your family's spiritual welfare than your own. No, the love of God, which will then be shed abroad in your hearts, will constrain you to do your utmost to preserve them: and the deep sense of God's free grace in Christ Jesus (which you will then have) in calling you, will excite you to do your utmost to save others, especially those of your own household.
>
> And though, after all your pious endeavors, some may continue unreformed, yet you will have this comfortable reflection to make, that you did what you could to make your families religious: and therefore may rest assured of sitting down in the kingdom of heaven, with Abraham, Joshua, and Cornelius, and all the godly householders, who in their several generations shone forth as so many lights in their respective households upon earth. Amen.[10]

PART THREE

MARRIAGE ENRICHMENT

EQUIPPING MEN TO LOVE THEIR WIVES AS CHRIST LOVED THE CHURCH

CHAPTER SEVEN

THE PURPOSE OF MARRIAGE

Being a family shepherd is not just about the way a man leads his children. It's also about the way he leads his wife. In fact, leading a wife is the foundation upon which a man's shepherding ministry in the home is built.

This is true because marriage is designed in such a way that, ideally, a man gets a wife before he gets children. Furthermore, whether or not God blesses a man with children, if he has a wife, he's still a family shepherd. It's also the case that once the children are gone, a man must continue to lead his home and shepherd his wife.

In other words, the attention you give your marriage is a huge part of being a family shepherd.

While it's a complete myth that half of all marriages end in divorce, the fact that marriages are weak and men and women are clueless as to how to make them strong is as real as it gets. Unfortunately, this is true inside as well as outside the church. This is crucial, since the first step for a man shepherding his family is to shepherd his wife. A strong marriage is the foundation upon which a strong family is built. And having a strong marriage requires a biblical understanding of the purposes for which God gave us the institution.

Moreover, understanding the purposes for which God designed marriage is foundational to shepherding a family. By understanding marriage in light of Christ, his cross, and his kingdom, a man will have no problem understanding the crucial nature of his own role as a husband and father. He'll also have a healthy balance between the weightiness of his task and potency of his provision.

PROCREATION

Procreation is the first and most obvious purpose for which God designed marriage. This goes back to the dominion mandate that we looked at earlier:

> And God blessed them. And God said to them, "Be fruitful and multiply and fill the earth and subdue it and have dominion over the fish of the sea and over the birds of the heavens and over every living thing that moves on the earth." (Gen. 1:28)

"Be fruitful and multiply" is often described as the very first command given to us in Scripture. However, that's technically not the case. As John Sailhamer points out, the subtlety of the Hebrew text is not to be overlooked: "The imperatives 'Be fruitful,' 'increase,' and 'fill' are not to be understood as commands in this verse since the introductory statement identifies them as a 'blessing.'"[1] In a sense, God's statement was like the father of the bride standing up at a wedding and saying, "May you be fruitful and multiply." The dominant idea here is that our fruitfulness is a blessing and not a burden.

Procreation viewed as a blessing is found not only in Genesis 1. The same sentiment is in Psalm 127:

> Behold, children are a heritage from the LORD,
>   the fruit of the womb a reward.
> Like arrows in the hand of a warrior
>   are the children of one's youth.
> Blessed is the man
>   who fills his quiver with them!
> He shall not be put to shame
>   when he speaks with his enemies in the gate. (Ps. 127:3–5)

Note the subtle distinction in the ESV: "Blessed is the man *who fills* his quiver with them." Compare this to KJV ("Happy is the man that hath his quiver full of them"), or NASB and NIV ("Blessed is the man whose quiver is full of them"). The ESV captures rather beautifully the sentiment behind the imperative. The idea is not that human beings are to reproduce at gunpoint. On the contrary, it's to be our delight.

To understand this, we have to view procreation as more than just having children. It is about the image of God being spread abroad throughout the earth. It's about desiring "godly offspring" (Mal. 2:15) and raising and discipling children to the glory of God (Deut. 6:1–15; see also Eph. 6:1–4). This is about one generation teaching the next about the wondrous deeds of the God of the covenant (Psalm 78).

This perspective changes our view of children completely. How can I neglect the discipleship of my children if I have such a view of the procreative purpose of marriage? How can I view my marriage through self-centered lenses?

SANCTIFICATION

Beyond the purpose of bearing, raising, and discipling children with a view toward expanding God's kingdom, he has also designed marriage to sanctify his people. This sanctification occurs both actively and passively.

ACTIVE SANCTIFICATION

By active sanctification, I mean those things God directs us to do in marriage with a view toward the sanctification of our spouse and ourselves. Let me share two primary examples.

First, the husband is called to love his wife as Christ loved the church, specifically for the purpose of her sanctification:

> Husbands, love your wives, as Christ loved the church and gave himself up for her, that he might sanctify her, having cleansed her by the washing of water with the word, so that he might present the church to himself in splendor, without spot or wrinkle or any such thing, that she might be holy and without blemish. (Eph. 5:25–27)

The husband is to work actively and purposefully toward his

wife's sanctification. The means alluded to here is Christ's example, "by the washing of water with the word." It's difficult to be certain about what precisely this phrase refers to; however, the idea is clear that the groom must actively seek the sanctification of his bride.[2]

Another example of active sanctification involves the marriage bed. God designed sex for more than just procreation. There's a sense in which the sexual relationship between a husband and wife is a weapon in the war against promiscuity and lust:

> Now concerning the matters about which you wrote: "It is good for a man not to have sexual relations with a woman." But because of the temptation to sexual immorality, each man should have his own wife and each woman her own husband. The husband should give to his wife her conjugal rights, and likewise the wife to her husband. For the wife does not have authority over her own body, but the husband does. Likewise the husband does not have authority over his own body, but the wife does. Do not deprive one another, except perhaps by agreement for a limited time, that you may devote yourselves to prayer; but then come together again, so that Satan may not tempt you because of your lack of self-control. (1 Cor. 7:1–5)

While this may not be the most "romantic" passage about marriage, it's important nonetheless. Here we see that God has "set apart" or sanctified the marriage bed.

Here in marriage, and here only, can men and women fulfill their God-given sexual desires in a God-honoring manner. Only in marriage do our sexual desires result in a glorious picture of the rapturous joy of the consummation yet to come between Christ and his bride. As a result, a healthy sexual relationship is a means by which Christians "save themselves for marriage" in a spiritual sense.

PASSIVE SANCTIFICATION

While active sanctification involves those things we do intentionally with a view toward sanctification for ourselves and our spouse, passive sanctification involves things that are unintentional. There are many ways in which I work to sanctify my wife without trying. When I forget to do something, God uses it to sanctify her. When I'm less than thoughtful and she has to be forgiving, God also uses that to sanctify her.

Consider Peter's admonition:

> Likewise, wives, be subject to your own husbands, so that even if some do not obey the word, they may be won without a word by the conduct of their wives, when they see your respectful and pure conduct. Do not let your adorning be external—the braiding of hair and the putting on of gold jewelry, or the clothing you wear—but let your adorning be the hidden person of the heart with the imperishable beauty of a gentle and quiet spirit, which in God's sight is very precious. For this is how the holy women who hoped in God used to adorn themselves, by submitting to their own husbands, as Sarah obeyed Abraham, calling him lord. And you are her children, if you do good and do not fear anything that is frightening. (1 Pet. 3:1–6)

This is most assuredly a sanctifying work.

God uses difficulties like those mentioned in 1 Peter to conform us to the image of his Son (Rom. 8:29). And husbands are not exempt from such passive sanctification:

> Likewise, husbands, live with your wives in an understanding way, showing honor to the woman as the weaker vessel, since they are heirs with you of the grace of life, so that your prayers may not be hindered. (1 Pet. 3:7)

Any man who has tried to "understand" his wife (or to understand any woman for that matter) knows it's a sanctifying work. However, most men don't think of it that way. In fact, many men see the difficulty inherent in understanding their wives as good reason to walk away.

Many men live under the faulty assumption that true marital bliss consists of being in a relationship with a woman who causes him little or no grief. As a result, many marriages find themselves in peril due to a failure to view their relationship as a sanctifying work. Family shepherds must grasp this truth. We must understand that God uses marriage to chisel away at our rough edges and to conform us to the image of his Son (Rom. 8:29).

Imagine God the Father doing surgery on you. Several things inside you must be removed, because they're contrary to the character of his Son, into whose image he's in the process of conforming you. One of the tools he's using in this process is your wife. You're impatient, so he gave you a woman who's very different than you are in order to work patience in you. You're selfish, so he gave you a woman who needs and depends on you.

As God continues to operate on you in this way, you suddenly jump up from the table intent on running away. "I'm done with this!" you proclaim, indignant over the pain and inconvenience of the process.

"Don't you love my Son?" God inquires.

"Of course I do. Jesus means everything to me."

Then you see the Father looking down at the tools with which he's conforming you to the image of the one you claim to love. Understanding the implication, you reply, "I know what you're trying to do. However, you're just going to have to find another way to do it."

Of course, this sounds absurd. Who among us would speak to the God of the universe in such a way? Who among us would express our love toward Christ by running away from something designed specifically to chisel away those aspects of our character that do not reflect his? Who among us, indeed!

A PICTURE OF SOMETHING MORE

In addition to procreation and sanctification, God also gave us marriage for the purpose of illustration. Marriage is a living, breathing picture of the relationship between Christ and his bride, the church. Understanding this truth is vitally important to the role of family shepherd.

First, the principle of illustration defines the family shepherd's *role*. Many family shepherds have a difficult time navigating the waters of marriage. Many blame their lack of an example from their own father, or worse, their lack of a father at all. Others look at the culture around them and wonder if it's even possible to be the leader of a godly marriage. These men keep wondering: How do I know what my role is as a husband? Do I look to my father? To my grandfather? Or how about to the culture at large? Even the church seems to have few exemplary marriages from which to draw.

However, there's one example that's perfect. Christ's example is the blueprint that shows every family shepherd what his role is in marriage. So whether we were raised in a godly Christian home or among pagans who disavowed marriage, we're never left in the dark.

Second, the principle of illustration defines the family shepherd's *goal*. Notice how that comes through in these words from Paul:

Husbands, love your wives, as Christ loved the church and gave himself up for her, that he might sanctify her, having cleansed her by the washing of water with the word, so that he might present the church to himself in splendor, without spot or wrinkle or any such thing, that she might be holy and without blemish. In the same way husbands should love their wives as their own bodies. He who loves his wife loves himself. For no one ever hated his own flesh, but nourishes and cherishes it, just as Christ does the church, because we are members of his body. "Therefore a man shall leave his father and mother and hold fast to his wife, and the two shall become one flesh." This mystery is profound, and I am saying that it refers to Christ and the church. However, let each one of you love his wife as himself, and let the wife see that she respects her husband. (Eph. 5:25–33)

The goal of the Good Shepherd is the sanctification of his bride by his selfless love. The goal of the family shepherd must therefore be the same. The goal is not self-gratification, but self-sacrifice with a view toward sanctification of the bride to the glory of the Father.

Third, the principle of illustration gives family shepherds *hope*. The fact that God has designed marriage as a representative picture of the union between Christ and the church shows that God will uphold marriage. The family shepherd who gives himself to the task of honoring God in his marriage can be assured of God's aid in the process, "for it is God who works in you, both to will and to work for his good pleasure" (Phil. 2:13). Certainly his good pleasure includes marriage, and he will be at work in that relationship on your behalf.

Having a proper perspective on the purposes of marriage will change the way a man views his role as a family shepherd. When I know that God designed the marriage covenant to sanctify both me and my wife, to paint a picture on earth of the relationship between Christ and his church and to bring forth a generation of kingdom citizens who will know and follow hard after God, then my perspective is altered completely.

Though my sin is ever before me, these truths call me back to the cross. Though my default position is to live for myself, these purposes remind me that I'm here to serve another.

As a husband, it's my duty to keep these truths forever before my eyes. As a pastor, it's my duty to keep them forever before the flock in both word and deed (1 Tim. 3:1–5; Titus 1:5–9; Phil. 2:13; 1 Pet. 5:2). This is indeed the foundation upon which the family shepherd's role is built. A man's role as the priest, prophet, provider, and protector of his household, as the discipler of his children, and as the visionary who blazes a trail for his family to follow flow from his role as a husband. And understanding his role as a husband begins with understanding God's purpose for marriage.

CHAPTER EIGHT

THE PRIMACY OF MARRIAGE

I've noticed an interesting phenomenon as I've traveled the country and talked to different people. No matter where I go, people consistently define or relate to men and women differently. When I talk to another man, he's eventually going to ask me what I *do*, since that's his way of defining both himself and others. However, if I talk to a woman, she'll eventually ask me who I'm *connected to*, since that's the way she defines herself and others. Men want to know about my job; women want to know about my wife and kids.

While this may seem subtle, it's actually very powerful. I think the women are actually on to something (as they usually are). I believe family shepherds would do well to change the way they look at who they are. And while we should all start with our relationship to God through his Son, Jesus Christ, our earthly identity should center much more around our role as family shepherds than around our role on the job.

JOHNSON VS. BAKER

The study of last names is quite fascinating. For example, last names, or surnames, did not appear in England until the eleventh century. As they developed, English surnames generally fell into four basic categories—trades, places, appearance, and kinship.[1] What I find interesting is that people in eleventh-century England were doing the same thing men do today, only more officially. What prompted a man to identify with his trade and become Mr. Baker—or Mr. Butler, Smith, Archer, Driver, Barber, Bishop, Brewer, or Leech (physician)—as opposed to identifying with his family and becoming Mr. John*son*, Wil*son*, Jami*son*, or Robin*son*?

While we're all stuck with the names that have been passed down to us by our ancestors, we still face the same decision. Are we as men going to be defined by our careers or by our families? I believe that as family shepherds we must opt for the latter.

Let me make clear that I realize we're all ultimately defined by our relationship to Christ. I'm not including that in the discussion here for two reasons: (1) Our identification as followers of Christ has no equal; neither my career nor my family is of equal value to my identification with my Lord; (2) What we're really discussing here is the *context* wherein we live out our identification with Christ.

As a follower of Christ, I'm called to live in numerous contexts (husband, father, employee, employer, student, citizen, etc.). What I'm getting at is how we prioritize those secondary contexts in our effort to serve the Lord day by day. With that in mind, let me state briefly why I believe that as our touchstone we should opt for our family (and particularly our marriage) as opposed to our career.

This part of the discussion is crucial, because when they identify that which defines and drives them, most men in our culture default to their careers. This is what determines where and when they move their families, how far away they live from extended family, the kind of church they attend (and how frequently), the lifestyle they enjoy, and the level of involvement they have in the discipleship of their children.

So a seismic shift is represented by changing the focus from one that says, "I'm a lawyer, and that defines the way my family is shaped," to one that says, "My wife and I entered a covenant relationship designed to bring forth, train, and launch a generation of godly offspring, and that's going to direct all the rest of my decisions." This isn't to say men should slack off at work. It is, however, to say that they should *not* slack off at home (something we almost never hear). This is a radical change of perspective, but one that I believe is warranted.

COVENANT VS. CONTRACT

The first reason we ought to identify ourselves primarily with our wives and not our careers is that our careers are fleeting, while our marriage is for life. It's fine for a man to have a number of careers. However, it's not acceptable for him to have the same approach to marriage. This truth echoes from the pen of the prophet Malachi: "So guard yourselves in your spirit, and let none of you be faithless to the wife of your youth" (Mal. 2:15).

This sounds like a simple thing, but it's much more complicated than we think. I'll never forget the day Colin Powell left the Bush Administration early in the second term. General Powell always fascinated me. I learned about him during the first Gulf War. He was an impressive man. As a young black college student majoring in international business, I considered him a bit of a hero. When he left the military and went into politics, I watched with eager anticipation. However, upon his resignation I found myself struggling to put the pieces together.

It wasn't his politics that gave me pause (though I'd come to realize that his position on key issues made him a man for whom I could probably never vote); rather, it was something he said. At sixty-seven years of age he gave a brief resignation speech and commented that he was going to devote more time to his family. Suddenly, his life flashed before my eyes. The general had given his life to the service of his country; now, when his children were all grown and gone, when there were no more games to go to or homework to help with or school plays to attend, he was shutting down his career to devote time to his family. How ironic!

By all accounts Colin Powell, like many men his age, had missed the times when he was needed most. Of course, I could be completely wrong. He could be the exception to the rule. Perhaps he made it to the pinnacle of his profession and gained international prominence while also devoting himself to his wife and children in unparalleled ways. But somehow, I doubt it.

In that moment when I heard Colin Powell make those comments, I also thought about myself. I was thirty-five years old at the time. Our older children (Jasmine and Trey) were eleven and fourteen, respectively. I was right in the midst of the storm. This was a gut check for me. Was I on the path to being a sixty-seven-year-old pastor whose grown children looked on as I resigned from a high-demand ministry position citing my desire to "spend more time with my family"? Would my children be filled with resentment and regret as they wondered why I didn't think about that when it mattered? I certainly hoped not.

But hoping wasn't going to make it so. I had to see myself first and foremost as Bridget's husband, and as her partner in raising, training, and launching arrows into the next generation. And then I had to simply let the rest of the pieces fall into place.

THE LESSER SERVES THE GREATER

A second reason we ought to identify ourselves primarily with our wives and not our careers is that our careers exist to serve our families (1 Tim. 5:8), not the other way around. My family doesn't exist to make me a better pastor, or writer, or businessman. My wife is not my suitable helper for the sake of my career advancement. In fact, wives are supposed to outlast careers, not the other way around. As a result, it's sheer folly to identify myself first and foremost with my career instead of with my wife.

This is at least in part what Paul has in mind in 1 Corinthians 7:

> I want you to be free from anxieties. The unmarried man is anxious about the things of the Lord, how to please the Lord. *But the married man is anxious about worldly things, how to please his wife*, and his interests are divided. (1 Cor. 7:32–34)

Are you anxious about how to please your wife? Note the marked difference between this and the idea that a man is defined first and foremost by his career. In the latter scenario, Eve's purpose as the perfect helper for Adam (Gen. 2:18) is shifted from that of a partner in the dominion mandate and the propagation of the *imago Dei* to nothing more than a bed warmer and a prop in Adam's gardening and animal-naming business. Certainly God had more than that in mind. Certainly Adam's relationship with Eve was central, not peripheral to his calling.

And if not before the fall, certainly the life of our first parents had a unified spiritual trajectory afterward as the entirety of redemptive history hinges on God's pronouncement in Genesis 3:15 and the coming Messiah who would reverse the curse. So no matter what Adam—or any other man for that matter—would do in his career, the big picture was to see the knowledge and worship of God spreading from generation to generation and throughout the earth, as God's plan of redemption unfolded.

And what about those of us on the other side of the coming of the Promised One? Do we now revert to some kind of career-based, fulfillment-oriented, achievement-driven existence (which was never man's purpose)? Absolutely not! Our privileged calling now is to live for the New Testament version of the dominion mandate—the Great Commission (Matt. 28:18–20). Therefore it would be sheer folly to define ourselves by our careers.

And for those who argue that the Great Commission would also negate such an emphasis on our marriages—not so fast! Remember, the very foundation upon which marriage is built is the relationship between the Redeemer and his redeemed (Eph. 5:22–32). It is not in my career, but in my marriage that I portray and proclaim these truths.

THE DANGER OF GETTING IT WRONG

Failure to grasp these truths has significant consequences. A man who fails to view his marriage properly, and who forsakes it for a career, will not only miss out on the glory and joy of his marriage; he'll also weaken his wife's hand as he asks her to handle a two-person job on her own.

Marriage is a glorious institution. The Bible is replete with references to the glory and joy of a man's relationship with his wife. "He who finds a wife finds a good thing and obtains favor from the Lord" (Prov. 18:22). "An excellent wife is the crown of her husband" (Prov. 12:4). "An excellent wife who can find? She is far more precious than jewels" (Prov. 31:10). What folly it would be to forsake something so precious for a fleeting career!

Again, this isn't to say a man cannot have a meaningful career. That's not the question. The question is, where's your foundation? Are you a doctor who has a wife on the side, or are you a husband and father who provides for his family through a job in the medical field?

Is it possible for a man who views his marriage as foundational to be a hardworking, effective physician (or lawyer, or brick mason, or policeman, or teacher)? Of course it is! And indeed this is what he must be. He should view his career as a means by which he can bring honor to God as he applies himself to the pursuit of truth and beauty in the application of his gifts, talents, and abilities in the kingdom of man. However, even this worthy pursuit takes a backseat to his marriage.

UNISON VS. UNION

Another reason it's wise for a man to view his marriage and not his job as foundational to his life is the biblical idea of union with his wife. We're called to work, but we're never called to be in union with our jobs. However, a man is most assuredly called to be in union with his wife.

For example, the Bible encourages us to "live with your wives in an understanding way, showing honor to the woman as the weaker vessel, since they are *heirs with you of the grace of life*, so that your prayers may not be hindered" (1 Pet. 3:7). What a beautiful picture of the union between a man and his wife! Can you imagine such a thing being said of a job?

First Peter is not the only place we see this truth spelled out. The apostle Paul puts an even finer point on the matter:

> In the same way husbands should love their wives as their own bodies. He who loves his wife loves himself. For no one ever hated his own flesh, but nourishes and cherishes it, just as Christ does the church, because we are members of his body. (Eph. 5:28–30)

Here we see the union between a man and his wife even more

clearly. And not only is the marriage relationship a union; it's a *one-flesh* union. More importantly, it's a living, breathing illustration of the one-flesh union between Christ and his church. How dare we forsake such a treasure, or relegate it to second-fiddle status for the sake of a job!

DEFINED BY YOUR MARRIAGE, NOT BY YOUR KIDS

Once a family shepherd grasps the primacy of his marriage in relation to his job, it becomes easier to see the primacy of his marriage in relation to his children. Nevertheless, this is a matter we must give attention to, since there's sometimes a tendency to prioritize our children to the neglect of our marriage.

There are at least three reasons that make prioritizing our children over our marriage both foolish and dangerous. First, our children will eventually leave home—and if they're the foundation of our family, then their departure will mean our family's demise. Second, our marriage forms the cornerstone of our children's security. Finally, one of our primary goals is to prepare our children for marriage.

PREPARING YOUR MARRIAGE FOR THE EMPTY NEST

I've had the unpleasant experience of witnessing the demise of several long-lived marriages. And while the demise of any marriage is unfortunate, there's something particularly disturbing when a couple divorces after decades of marriage. Interestingly, these couples actually tend not to agree with that assessment. They believe that "since the children are no longer at home," their actions will have less severe consequences. That's a debatable issue, but it's not the point here. What their rationalization reveals is a major cause of their marriage's demise—they prioritized their children over their marriage.

To my knowledge, I've never talked to a person who divorced after twenty-five or thirty years who *didn't* say something like this: "Once the kids were gone, we realized we really didn't have much of a marriage." This realization, coupled with the mistaken idea that they did something heroic by waiting until the children were all out of the house to commence with the unpleasant proceedings, speaks volumes about their priorities. The consistent refrain is, "We did it all for the kids." How tragic!

Building a marriage on the foundation of the preeminence of children is like building a house on a rented removable slab. You may have days or even years when you feel completely secure, but the day is coming when the lease will be up and the foundation upon which your home stands will be taken away. A family shepherd must not allow his family to fall into this trap.

PROVIDING YOUR CHILDREN WITH SECURITY

Ironically, those who prioritize their children above their marriage are not only jeopardizing their marriage, they're actually depriving their children of the very thing they desire to provide them. The greatest source of security our children have in this world is a God-honoring, Christ-centered marriage between their parents.

Putting the children first is like a police officer putting away his badge and gun in order to make the public feel more at ease. But it's only a matter of time before the things this officer has forsaken become the very things he needs for doing his job; he must provide these things in reality, not just in sentiment.

Likewise a family shepherd must put his marriage before his children in order to provide them with the security they both need and desire.

PREPARING YOUR CHILDREN FOR MARRIAGE

Finally, prioritizing your children above your marriage is both foolish and dangerous because it sets a precedent that contradicts one of the greatest lessons you'll ever teach your children—how to be good husbands and wives. We must first and foremost model a commitment to marriage. Failure to do this will communicate ideas that are contrary to what we believe—starting with the narcissism it tends to create in our children—including the pitfalls that may follow them into their marriage.

For example, if we prioritize our children above our marriage, we teach our children that marriage exists for children. If this is the case, how will our children react to the early months or years of their marriage when there are no children? How will they respond if, God forbid, they should struggle with infertility? If the heart of marriage is "living for the kids," these scenarios could be difficult at best.

Jesus our Savior—and our example of what a bridegroom truly is—laid down his life for his bride (Eph. 5:25). He doesn't neglect her for another. And it's this relationship of our Savior to his bride that governs our understanding of our role as husbands and family shepherds. We must give ourselves to and for our wives. We must view them not only as *ours* but as *us*!

As I often remind myself concerning my wife, "She's not just mine; she's *me*. She's bone of my bones and flesh of my flesh (Gen. 2:23); she's my body (Eph. 5:28–29), and I am her head (1 Cor. 11:3; Eph. 5:23). We are *one* (Eph. 5:31; see also Gen. 2:24); and our union is a blessing to our children (1 Cor. 7:14)."

As family shepherds, our primary mission is to love our wives as our own selves. We must not allow anything to interfere with this mission. Neither our careers nor our children can be allowed to keep us from our task of modeling for the world the beautiful, mysterious, one-flesh union of our Savior and his bride (Eph. 5:33).

CHAPTER NINE

MALE HEADSHIP IN THE HOME

This chapter ought to be a given. The very term *family shepherd* assumes that a man is the head of his household. However, there are few things contested more hotly in the church and the culture at large today. This one ranks right up there with spanking (we'll look at that one in chapter 12), although I would argue that since in one sense spanking is offensive *because* it's the exercise of parental authority and headship, the issue of headship is actually more hotly contested.

The Bible teaches male headship in the home in a number of places, including Ephesians 5:21–33; Colossians 3:18–19; 1 Peter 3:1–7; and Titus 2:5. But it's the first three chapters of Genesis that serve as the theological foundation for the matter. In fact, when Paul argues for male headship in the church in 1 Timothy 2:12–13, he bases his argument on the Genesis account. Paul sees Adam's headship in the garden of Eden as the basis for male headship today in the church and the home.

The issue for Paul in marriage is not who's smarter, stronger, or more important; for him, as well as for the other biblical writers, the question is one of God-ordained order. Thus Paul declares that "the head of every man is Christ, the head of a wife is her husband, and the head of Christ is God" (1 Cor. 11:3). This is a crucial point. If male headship is merely a preference, we have no right to argue for it as an essential element of family shepherding. If, however, it's a truth based on God's decree and design, we have no right to argue for anything else.

Despite all this, there are plenty of objections to male headship in the home, and the objections come from within the church as well as outside it. And just as it is important to address the objections to spanking in order to alleviate the hesitancy some men may feel about it, it's important for the same reason to address the many objections to male headship in the home.

It is important to address the objections to male headship because some are really objections to the *abuse* of male headship. Unfortunately, ignorance, inaccurate teaching, poor examples, and plain old sin have led many men to fall into practices that don't resemble the biblical model at all. As a result, any effort to equip family shepherds must include painting an accurate portrait of biblical headship—beginning with answering objections, both legitimate and otherwise.

OBJECTIONS FROM INSIDE THE CHURCH

Gilbert Bilezikian's book *Beyond Sex Roles* and Gordon Fee's commentary on 1 Corinthians are two of the seminal works in evangelical feminism.[1] For our purposes, we'll be examining Bilezikian's main objections. My goal is not to offer a comprehensive examination of evangelical feminism, but to lay out the main arguments so you're aware of them and know how to respond.

I assure you that this isn't just an academic, ivory-tower debate. Feminist ideas have seeped into most local churches. The influence of these objections has always carried much weight because of God's words to Eve after the fall: "Your desire shall be for your husband, and he shall rule over you" (Gen. 3:16). The verse refers not to sensual passion and affection, but to anger and resentment. In fact, the idea appears again in the very next chapter of Genesis, giving us a clearer understanding of the meaning. God says to Cain, "Sin is crouching at the door. Its desire is for you, but you must rule over it" (Gen. 4:7). Thus, in Genesis 3:16 it's this "desire"—this resentment of male headship—that's a product of the fall. Consequently, fallen man is always looking for an excuse to avoid male headship. And since Christians aren't completely free from all the effects of sin this side of glorification (see Rom. 7:15–23), it appeals to our flesh as well.

Numerous places in the Bible teach male headship, but the key battleground is Ephesians 5. As Daniel Doriani notes:

> Because Ephesians 5 appears so obviously to contradict their views, feminist interpreters are obligated to attend to it. Unless they are willing to renounce their feminism, evangelical feminists must argue that despite its apparent clarity, Ephesians 5 fails to endorse male headship and perhaps even undermines it.[2]

As the seminal biblical text concerning male headship, Ephesians 5 is therefore also the main target of the evangelical feminist opposition.

Evangelical feminists offer three main arguments in response to Ephesians 5.[3] First, they argue that Paul's injunction was temporary. Second, they argue that male headship was a result of the curse (and thus is no longer applicable to believers). Third, they argue that Ephesians 5:21 calls for mutual submission and therefore essentially cancels out any understanding of what follows that would place the husband in authority over his wife.

Again, our goal here is simple. We want family shepherds to be aware of the objections and respond appropriately, so please understand and bear with my brevity, as we take up the main objections one by one.

EPHESIANS 5 IS A TEMPORARY INJUNCTION

"That was cultural." Oh, to have a dollar for every time I've heard that familiar refrain. While it's true that many things in the Bible are difficult to apply because their cultural setting and nuance is so foreign to us, it's a stretch to apply that to Ephesians 5 without, in essence, agreeing that any and all moral teaching in the New Testament is culturally tainted and therefore open to whatever radical reinterpretation happens to fit our modern fancy. [4] Family shepherds need to be ready to deal with this misguided yet popular objection.

EPHESIANS 5 IS A RESULT OF THE CURSE

Though the logic in this version of the argument against male headship is tortured, evangelical feminists employ it nonetheless. Daniel Doriani summarizes Aida Spencer's thoughts on this to illustrate the point:

> Her curse now was to be ruled, perversely to long for her husband and he to rule over her. She would want to be dominated by her husband and he would submit[!] to this desire. God does not command Adam to rule or govern his wife. Rather the curse is Eve's. The ruling is a consequence of Eve's longing and her fall.[5]

We must reject such logic, as well as the type of damage this interpretation does to the text.

First, Spencer's rendering of Genesis 3:16 is completely novel. As I've already noted, interpreting the meaning of the words in Genesis 3:16 isn't difficult in light of the parallel use in 4:7 (see above). If Spencer is right, then sin longed to be dominated by Cain! Moreover, this reading again ignores the fact that Adam's headship was established in Genesis 2 *before* the fall.

Second, Spencer's logic simply doesn't add up. If male headship is a product of the curse that can then be done away with in Christ, then so too should pain in childbearing for Christian women be done away with, along with thorns and thistles and arduous work for men.

Ironically, a better interpretation would view Spencer's argument as a manifestation of the curse. The woman's "desire" is to be rid of male headship—but there's no way out. It's a part of the created order, and no amount of tortured logic will change that.

Family shepherds must hold fast in the face of such attacks.

EPHESIANS 5 HAS BEEN MISUNDERSTOOD UNTIL NOW

The final objection evangelical feminists offer is the idea that Paul's words have been misinterpreted or misunderstood until recent days. The crux of their argument centers on Ephesians 5:21, where Paul admonishes believers concerning "submitting to one another out of reverence for Christ." However, Paul's statement in verse 21 comes at the end of a paragraph (5:15–21).[6] Thus, 5:21 is an introductory statement that explains submission of believers in three contexts—wives to husbands (5:22–33), children to parents (6:1–4), and slaves to masters (6:5–9).

Much more could be said (and a great deal has been written on the topic by several authors), but I want to emphasize that it's important for us as family shepherds to simply be aware of these objections for several reasons. First, we must know what we believe about the matter if we're going to exercise the headship to which we are called. Second, we need to be prepared to give an answer (1 Pet. 3:15). Finally, we must be prepared to explain to our children why our family operates the way it does in light of what has become an increasingly egalitarian Christian mainstream.

OBJECTIONS FROM OUTSIDE THE CHURCH

In addition to answering the critics within the church, we must also be ready to respond to those on the outside. There we don't face disparate interpretations of key texts, but the presentation and living out of a worldview entirely different from our own.

Feminism is at war with male headship. Radical feminist Andrea Dworkin sounded the alarm in 1986:

> Sisters: I don't know who you are, or how many, but I will tell you what happened to us. We were brave and we were fools; some of us collaborated; I don't know the outcome. It is late 1986 now, and we are losing. The war is men against women; the country is the United States.[7]

This war has, for the most part, been a propaganda war. Dworkin's writings, like that of many leading feminists, are filled with dramatic overstatements, unfounded statistics, and outright falsehoods. However, the feminists' side has won the day in academia, politics, the media, and (in some cases) the church. These women (and sometimes men) are not to be ignored.

From the feminists, we'll generally face opposition on two

fronts: inequality and abuse. As stated earlier, it's not enough to merely dismiss these objections, since they would have little or no traction unless there was a kernel of truth in them. We not only deal with the natural tendency of fallen man to reject male headship (women through rebellion and men through passivity); we also have the added impetus of living examples that bolster the opposition's case.

INEQUALITY

The first and most pervasive objection traditional feminists offer is that male headship is wrong because it relegates women to second-class status. Feminist Robin Morgan, whose website touts her as "an invited speaker at every major university in North America,"[8] sums up this sentiment well: "We can't destroy the inequities between men and women until we destroy marriage."[9] For feminists, it's not only male headship, but the very institution of marriage that's at fault:

> The nuclear family must be destroyed, and people must find better ways of living together. . . . Whatever its ultimate meaning, the break-up of families now is an objectively revolutionary process. . . . No woman should have to deny herself any opportunities because of her special responsibilities to her children. . . . Families will be finally destroyed only when a revolutionary social and economic organization permits people's needs for love and security to be met in ways that do not impose divisions of labor, or any external roles, at all.[10]

How, then, does a family shepherd respond to these charges and lead his family in such a way that there's no room for anyone to legitimately say he manifests such qualities?

First, we must have a biblical view of the equality between men and women. Second, know that the best response is an accurate expression of the biblical reality. For in that reality, God makes it clear that men and women are equal from the beginning:

> Then God said, "Let us make man in our image, after our likeness.
> And let them have dominion over the fish of the sea and over the

birds of the heavens and over the livestock and over all the earth and over every creeping thing that creeps on the earth." (Gen. 1:26)

So then, how does one hold to the complete equality of men and women and to male headship in marriage? Ray Ortlund sums it up succinctly: "In the partnership of two spiritually equal human beings . . . the man bears the primary responsibility to lead the partnership in a God-glorifying direction."[11]

We do not have to concede that there is headship only in the midst of inequality. This is patently false. The Bible makes it clear that Christ is equal to the Father in every way (John 1:1; 5:18; 10:33; 2 Cor. 4:4; Phil. 2:6; Col. 1:15, 19; 2:9), and yet there is headship even in the Trinity—a point that Paul brings in as he also discusses the headship of husbands in the home:

> I want you to understand that the head of every man is Christ, the head of a wife is her husband, and the head of Christ is God. (1 Cor. 11:3)

This may seem like an esoteric matter, but I assure you there's nothing more practical for a family shepherd. If we doubt our place, we'll eventually doubt our purpose. On the other hand, knowing our position is the first step to embracing our assignment.

ABUSE

The idea that the practice of male headship will lead inevitably to abuse is ubiquitous in feminist circles. In fact, many leading feminists go so far as to call all heterosexual sex rape.[12] Though in a less volatile setting, even distinguished professor of linguistics Suzette Elgin writes that the concept of male headship "requires violence in the same way that human beings require oxygen."[13] And Elgin is no man-hating spinster. She's twice-married (marrying again after the death of her first husband), and the mother of five!

Andrea Dworkin goes even further:

> Under patriarchy, no woman is safe to live her life, or to love, or to mother children. Under patriarchy, every woman is a victim, past, present, and future. Under patriarchy, every woman's daughter is a

victim, past, present, and future. Under patriarchy, every woman's son is her potential betrayer and also the inevitable rapist or exploiter of another woman.[14]

While these statements are astonishing, we must remember that they go virtually unchallenged in our politically correct society, and have gained much ground among younger women. Therefore, we must respond to them. But fear not—God hasn't left us wanting.

The biblical view of male headship is as much opposed to the abuse of women as the feminists themselves claim to be. However, unlike feminists who, for example, will rarely come to the aid of a conservative Christian woman, the biblical model isn't bound by political allegiances; instead it views all women as worthy of respect, honor, and protection. Ray Ortlund said it best: "The antithesis to male headship is male domination."[15]

This of course is also the essence of Peter's admonition: "Husbands, live with your wives in an understanding way, showing honor to the woman as the weaker vessel, since they are heirs with you of the grace of life, so that your prayers may not be hindered" (1 Pet. 3:7). And Paul urges husbands to "love their wives as their own bodies" (Eph. 5:28).

AN OLD WAR WITH A NEW TWIST

Feminism's war on male headship is neither new nor surprising. In fact, male headship was at the very center of the spiritual battle that resulted in the fall of man recorded for us in Genesis, as John Piper and Wayne Grudem explain:

> We think that Satan's main target was not Eve's peculiar gullibility (if she had one), but rather Adam's headship as the one ordained by God to be responsible for the life of the garden. Satan's subtlety is that he knew the created order God had ordained for the good of the family, and he deliberately defied it by ignoring the man and taking up his dealings with the woman. Satan put her in the position of spokesman, leader, and defender. At that moment both the man and the woman slipped from their innocence and let

themselves be drawn into a pattern of relating that to this day has proved destructive.[16]

Whether that battle takes the form of novel evangelical interpretations of key biblical texts, or of propaganda from radical feminists, in the end it all boils down to the serpent slithering up to the woman with the sinister words, "Did God actually say . . . ?" (Gen. 3:1). Only now we know how to answer. Moreover, we know that Jesus Christ, the seed of the woman, has crushed the serpent's head (Gen. 3:15).

It is Christ's headship that is ultimately being questioned, since the headship of the man in marriage is merely an expression of the heavenly reality (Eph. 5:22–24). Therefore, encouraging men to reject their rightful role is about much more than changing the way we view "gender roles"; it goes to the heart of what we believe about the gospel. As a result, family shepherds cannot afford to be passive in this matter. We must counter objections and strive to live in accordance with God's precepts, regardless of the cost.

PART FOUR

THE TRAINING AND DISCIPLINE OF CHILDREN

EQUIPPING MEN TO RAISE KINGDOM-MINDED WARRIORS

CHAPTER TEN

REMEMBERING THE FALL

"It is with our sins," declared the nineteenth-century Scottish author and pastor Horatius Bonar, "that we go to God, for we have nothing else to go with that we can call our own. This is one of the lessons that we are so slow to learn; yet without learning this we cannot take one right step in that which we call a religious life."[1]

While most Christians would agree wholeheartedly with Bonar, few would recognize his statement as a foundation for shepherding a family. Nevertheless, it is crucial to our task as family shepherds. We must have a grasp on our children's greatest need if we ever hope to see it met. And once we do understand this issue correctly, our response will not be manipulative techniques, but the gospel of grace.

Rare is the man who views his discipline and instruction of his children through the lens of the gospel. For the most part, our approach to parenting resembles more closely that of Dr. Phil, Dr. Spock, or Dr. Oprah than it does Dr. Bonar. The reason? Our theology.

Most men are completely unaware of the impact their theology has on their parenting. This is a fact that cannot be ignored when it comes to equipping family shepherds. Failure to address such fundamental issues will eventually lead to great harm. At the very least, there will be much more confusion and frustration than necessary, and perhaps less hope and dependence than is called for.

Like most other theological issues of great importance, it's useful to turn to the theologian's theologian, Augustine. This great warrior fought many a theological battle in the fourth and fifth centuries, but "of all the disputes in which Augustine was engaged, that with the Pelagians was the most famous."[2] The battle between Augustine and Pelagius, contrary to popular belief, was not just about explaining how people are saved. It was a clash between two radically different understandings of humanity.

Augustine saw mankind as entirely in need of God's grace and mercy—as epitomized in a prayer to the Lord that he wrote in his *Confessions*: "Give what you command, and command what you will." These words reflected man's ultimate dependence on God "for courage, strength, and ability to do his will."[3]

But Pelagius found Augustine's prayer to be repulsive. Although he was living at the time in the morally corrupt city of Rome, Pelagius believed human beings already possessed the full capacity to carry out God's will, "including the capacity not to sin"; in his view, human beings "do not have any internal tendency to sin; they are not inclined toward doing evil. . . . There is no sinful nature in people when they are born."[4]

In response, Augustine carefully explained that "as a result of Adam's fall, humanity lost the freedom of will it once enjoyed. . . . Indeed, rather than being *able not to sin,* all people after the fall are *not able not to sin.* . . . Clearly this was the complete opposite of Pelagius's position."[5]

Here was a pitched battle of worldviews; these were fundamental, essential, nonnegotiable issues. As B. B. Warfield noted in the last century,

> There are at bottom but two types of religious thought in the world— if we may improperly use the term "religious" for both of them. There is the religion of faith; there is the "religion" of works. Calvinism [developed from Augustinianism] is the pure embodiment of the former of these; what is known in Church History as Pelagianism is the pure embodiment of the latter of them. All other forms of "religious" teaching which have been known in Christendom are but unstable attempts at compromise between the two.[6]

His words echoed an earlier assessment by the American Presbyterian leader A. A. Hodge: "There are, in fact . . . but two complete self-consistent systems of Christian theology possible"; these were "Augustinianism completed in Calvinism" on one hand, and Pelagianism on the other, with semi-Pelagianism (or Arminianism) coming between them "as the system of compromises" between the two.[7]

Let me say up front that I realize few Christians would identify with strict Pelagianism. However, few would also identify with Augustinian/Calvinistic theology as well. Most choose the much-lauded middle ground, or simply stick their heads in the sand and ignore the issue altogether. After all, "doctrine divides." And while I don't have time to argue against the validity of such a compromise, I assure you this mini-excursus is necessary. My goal here is to demonstrate the prevalence in our Christian culture today of Pelagian, or at least Semi-Pelagian doctrine, and how this influences the way we view child training.

First, let's put a little more meat on the bones and try to get a better grasp on the basic assumptions of Pelagianism so that we can see its effect on our ideas about raising children. This time we look at the words of Charles Hodge (the father of A. A. Hodge, whom I quoted above); this selection is from his highly influential *Systematic Theology*, as he explains Pelagianism's view of humanity:

> According to Pelagians . . . man was created a rational free agent, but without moral character. He was neither righteous nor unrighteous, holy nor unholy. He had simply the capacity of becoming either. Being endowed with reason and free will, his character depended upon the use which he made of those endowments. If he acted right, he became righteous; if he acted wrong, he became unrighteous.[8]

Man, the "rational free agent," is seen in such a perspective as essentially good, or at least neutral morally. We have the capacity to choose righteousness, and that choice is what separates Christians from non-Christians.

On the other hand, the Augustinian/Calvinistic position posits that man is fallen and utterly incapable of any good—a view supported by passages such as Jeremiah 13:23, Romans 3:10–18, and

Psalms 14:1–3 and 53:1–3. This position does *not* hold that men do not do some things that are good outwardly, but that they are not good *ultimately*, or in any meritorious or efficacious sense.

So what does all this have to do with the way we train up our children? Everything! There are myriad books out there on child training, and most of them are written from a Semi-Pelagian, behaviorist perspective (typically influenced by the twentieth-century psychologists B. F. Skinner, Carl Rogers, and Carl Jung). The seminal example of the influence of Pelagian/Semi-Pelagian theology and behaviorist psychology in child training is Michael Pearl's book, *To Train Up a Child*. I'm ashamed to say that we even had a copy of this book on our church book table for a while (before I actually familiarized myself with Pearl's work).

In a classic example of the application of Pelagianism in child training, Pearl writes:

> At their creation, Adam and Eve were complete physically, but *morally undeveloped*. A four-month fetus, still in the mother's womb, is a living soul. Though all of its tiny members match those of a mature adult, it is yet *an incomplete creation needing further growth before becoming distinct from its mother*. In like manner, a three-year-old child, in its soul, has all the tiny features of a morally responsible adult— a knowledge of right and wrong, a sense of justice, accountability, conscience, duty, guilt, shame, etc. *Yet, none of the moral faculties are developed to the point of being fully operative and independent. The child is not a morally viable soul. He is an incomplete moral being.* He is not accountable. Morally, the three-year-old is still in the womb. Moral life begins its development sometime after birth, probably in the second or third year, and continues until it matures about ten to fifteen years of age.[9]

Did you catch that? He referred to the child as an "incomplete creation," and "not a morally viable soul." This is Pelagianism 101! Remember that Charles Hodge, whom I quoted above, wrote his *Systematic Theology* over one hundred years earlier, though it appears that Pearl's quote is precisely what Hodge had in mind when he penned those words.

But wait—there's more. Pearl adds this:

Observation seems to suggest that some children may be account-able as early as five, while others may not be fully accountable un-til nineteen. The mentally impaired may never develop to the point of moral responsibility . . . moral development is a process, and the small child is not yet a viable moral soul. All child training must be administered with that firmly in mind.[10]

This perspective doesn't necessarily lead to behaviorism as the natural outgrowth. One could just as easily conclude that the child's moral neutrality requires psychoanalysis, gestalt therapy, or a twelve-step program. Or—though this would be a stretch—I guess Pearl could conclude that the answer is a heavy dose of the gospel in an effort to fill the void with the right "stuff."

However, Pearl, far from employing a gospel-centered ap-proach, introduces classic behaviorism as the appropriate re-sponse to this moral neutrality. He writes, "Before [a child] can decide to do good, his parents must CONDITION him to do good."[11] Hence, "doing good" is something that one can accomplish apart from Christ through proper conditioning. This is a direct contra-diction to Jesus's teaching:

I am the true vine, and my Father is the vinedresser. Every branch in me that does not bear fruit he takes away, and every branch that does bear fruit he prunes, that it may bear more fruit. Already you are clean because of the word that I have spoken to you. Abide in me, and I in you. As the branch cannot bear fruit by itself, unless it abides in the vine, neither can you, unless you abide in me. I am the vine; you are the branches. Whoever abides in me and I in him, he it is that bears much fruit, for *apart from me you can do nothing*. If anyone does not abide in me he is thrown away like a branch and withers; and the branches are gathered, thrown into the fire, and burned. (John 15:1–6)

And lest Pearl be taken out of context, allow me to draw your attention to an incontrovertible example of his theological per-spective:

There will come a time when your child must stand alone before the "the tree of the knowledge of good and evil." As the purpose of God has permitted, he will inevitably partake of the forbidden fruit. Now, in the developing years, you can make a difference in how he will re-spond after he has "eaten." Will he opt for Adam and Eve's fig-leaf cov-ering, or God's sacrificial covering? Will he hide his sin, or repent?[12]

Again, this is a popular Christian parenting book! There's al-most no need to explain the depth of unbiblical teaching here. Pearl denies original sin outright. One is almost not surprised when he ends the chapter with this jaw-dropping statement: "You can begin the child's 'sanctification' long before his salvation."[13]

The result is a child-training approach that relies on behavioral modification as opposed to spiritual transformation. Instead of the child's greatest need being the gospel, his greatest need is a parent whose "role is not like that of policemen, but more like that of the Holy Spirit," since the child is "incapable of holding moral values." Hence, repetition, correction, and conditioning are the hallmarks of Pearl's "method."

The influence of Pearl's work in certain circles cannot be over-estimated. This is especially true in homeschooling families, which constitute the lion's share of the households in many family integrated congregations. Accordingly, I am well aware of the con-sequences of his influence.

INCOMPLETE MORAL BEING—OR VIPER IN A DIAPER?

Contrast Pearl's approach with that of Tedd Tripp, an author, theo-logian, counselor, and pastor: "A change in behavior that does not stem from a change in heart is not commendable; it is *condem-nable*."[14] From Tripp's perspective, our children are not morally neutral or incomplete beings; they're sinners. As the psalmist ex-claims, "I was brought forth in iniquity, and in sin did my mother conceive me" (Ps. 51:5).

Human sinfulness is a fact from which there's simply no hon-est escape:

> Therefore, just as sin came into the world through one man, and
> death through sin, and so death spread to all men because all

sinned. . . . Therefore, as one trespass led to condemnation for all men, so one act of righteousness leads to justification and life for all men. For as by the one man's disobedience the many were made sinners, so by the one man's obedience the many will be made righteous. (Rom. 5:12, 18–19)

We must therefore view the gospel, not behaviorism, as the "central focus of parenting," as Tripp encourages us to do:

> You need to direct not simply the behavior of your children, but the attitudes of their hearts. You need to show them not just the "what" of their sin and failure, but the "why." Your children desperately need to understand not only the external "what" they did wrong, but also the internal "why" they did it. You must help them see that God works from the inside out. Therefore your parenting goal cannot simply be well behaved children. Your children must also understand why they sin and how to recognize internal change.[15]

In short, our children must learn that they're sinners. They didn't simply "pick up bad habits"; they *sin*. As noted by the nineteenth-century Scottish Presbyterian Robert Shaw in his commentary on the Westminster Confession of Faith,

> The universal prevalence of sin cannot be accounted for, as Pelagians have alleged, by the influence of bad example. . . . There are manifestations of moral depravity so very early in childhood as to anticipate all capacity for observing and following the example of others.[16]

To think otherwise, as we see in the behaviorist approach, leads to a style of parenting that's anything but gospel-centered. As family shepherds, we must have a right view of our child's problem if we're to have a right view of the solution.

FOCUS ON CHARACTER

Starting with a right understanding of our child's problem will lead to a right assessment of our child's need. This in turn will result in right motives and methods in addressing those needs. Ultimately, this takes us beyond our child's need for right behavior to their need for a right heart and right character. As Tedd Tripp writes, "Addressing the child's character places the emphasis on issues of the heart. It enables you to get underneath the behavior and address the thoughts, motives, and purposes of the heart."[17]

Unfortunately, most fathers think very little about issues like the Augustinian-Pelagian debate. We opt instead for the latest how-to fads and programs that just "give us the facts." Consequently, we end up adopting practices that are at best unhealthy, and at worst, heretical. We end up teaching our children a theology through our practices that will be very difficult to overcome with our later explanations of theory or philosophy, since much more is caught than taught.

Some men will say, "Let's just use the behaviorist material while exercising cautious wisdom with it. Surely we can eat the meat and spit out the bones." However, there are two major problems with this approach to equipping family shepherds. First, we live in a broken culture. Few fathers in our day have the theological wherewithal to sift through a book like Michael Pearl's *To Train Up a Child* and see, let alone correct, the theological errors there. Most men will simply get bogged down in the practical application and success stories long enough to see some changes—which they *will* see, since the behavioral approach is built on methods that are successful in training animals—while failing to recognize the works-righteousness they're fostering in both themselves and their children.

Second, there are much better books to help in parenting than those like Michael Pearl's. It's true that there are no perfect books; if there were, we'd have no need for new ones. However, many books do a good job of laying out a biblical pattern and applying it faithfully to the matter at hand.[18]

Moreover, there are different types of error. It's more desirable to deal with minor errors or differences (often based on differences derived from very close readings of difficult texts) from a like-minded brother with a shared worldview than to wade through fundamental differences in search of the occasional nugget.

So as we go forward, let's remember that theology matters. You don't get right orthopraxy from bad orthodoxy. A true family shepherd must be a man of the Word—a man of theology and doctrine. The man who desires to lead the family he loves must also be a true lover of the Lord's Word.

CHAPTER ELEVEN

FORMATIVE DISCIPLINE

What may be my favorite book on the Christian family begins with these words:

> As the great God, who at the beginning said, "Let us make man after our image," has made man a sociable creature, so it is evident that families are the nurseries of all societies. . . . When families are under ill discipline, all other societies, being ill-disciplined as a result, will feel that error.[1]

The book is entitled *A Family Well-Ordered,* and the author is Cotton Mather, a great Puritan force in colonial America. It's barely fifty pages long, but every page drips with Spirit-filled, soul-stirring, convicting, encouraging, eye-opening biblical truths. I must confess that I weep nearly every time I read it. In this age where family worship has been replaced by ballet practice, soccer games, baseball leagues, and television, Mather's words are more poignant than ever.

Try as I might, I cannot write a chapter about formative discipline without referring to Mather's book extensively.[2] I'll follow his outline, since I dare not try to improve upon it.

Mather wrote during a time when family worship was the norm. However, he and the people he pastored faced the same problem we all do: their children, like ours, were born in sin. As a result, these fathers and mothers needed to be instructed and encouraged to parent with purpose, always keeping eternity in view.

Mather also wrote in a time that knew nothing of the behaviorism on the one extreme, and the passivism on the other, that dominate so much thinking about parenting in our day.[3] Mather's approach was neither to treat children like machines that respond to input and stimuli reminiscent of Pavlov's dog, nor to view them as autonomous, self-directed beings who need merely to be left alone to explore and eventually figure things out on their own. Mather's approach was centered on the gospel. He saw children as made in the image of God, yet fallen, and he viewed parenting as a spiritual exercise.

The following six principles from Mather form the basis for an effective approach to formative discipline.[4]

CONSIDER THE CONDITION OF YOUR CHILDREN

Mather asks parents,

> Do you not know that your children have precious and immortal souls within them? They are not all flesh. You who are the parents of their flesh must know that your children have spirits also.[5]

As a father, I resonate with the apostle John's words: "I have no greater joy than to hear that my children are walking in the truth" (3 John 4). However, like every family shepherd, I struggle with the tendency to prioritize and concentrate on other pursuits. We must remember that there's nothing more "real" or more consequential than the fact that our children are immortal souls who must stand one day before God.

Have you ever considered this? When you look into the eyes of your children, do you mostly see a future doctor, lawyer, or linebacker? Or do you see a person who'll spend eternity in either heaven or hell? Do you see a soul that must bow the knee to Christ?

John Wesley captured this critical reality in a sermon on family religion, where he described children as

> immortal spirits whom God hath, for a time, entrusted to your care, that you may train them up in all holiness, and fit them for the enjoyment of God in eternity. This is a glorious and important trust; seeing one soul is of more value than all the world beside. Every child, therefore, you are to watch over with the utmost care, that, when you are called to give an account of each to the Father of Spirits, you may give your accounts with joy and not with grief.[6]

To be faithful to this "glorious and important trust" requires the kind of formative discipline that's about more than teaching our children how to "behave." Our goal must be more meaningful than that.

Formative discipline begins with the reality that our children's greatest need is regeneration; that understanding will lead to parenting that goes beyond the behaviorism of Skinner and Rogers and Jung (which unfortunately has been the basis of much child-training advice in recent decades). Johnny doesn't disobey because he's cranky, tired, or hungry, or because he hasn't been conditioned properly; he does it because he's a descendent of Adam.

INSTRUCT YOUR CHILDREN IN THE GREAT MATTERS OF SALVATION

Mather counsels parents,

> Instruct your children in the articles of religion, and acquaint them with God, Christ, the mysteries of the gospel, and the doctrine and methods of the great salvation.[7]

Knowing that our children need Christ is only half the battle. We must also help our children recognize this great matter for themselves. We must "*instruct* them," so that, as Wesley put it, we "take care that every person who is under our roof have all such knowledge as is necessary to salvation."[8] This again is crucial to formative discipline. We're not merely managing our children's behavior; we're actually instructing them in righteousness.

The next time you find yourself at the end of your rope with that child who just doesn't seem to get it, remember that his greatest need is the gospel. The next time those two daughters of yours quarrel, don't ask them what happened; tell them! Remind them of the essential reason for their disagreement, and that God knows exactly why they don't get along:

> What causes quarrels and what causes fights among you? Is it not this, that your passions are at war within you? You desire and do not have, so you murder. You covet and cannot obtain, so you fight and

> quarrel. You do not have, because you do not ask. You ask and do
> not receive, because you ask wrongly, to spend it on your passions.
> (James 4:1–3)

And what's the solution? Is it that they need to learn to share? Perhaps. But there's a deeper issue, one that gets to our need for repentance and dependence on God:

> Submit yourselves therefore to God. Resist the devil, and he will flee
> from you. Draw near to God, and he will draw near to you. Cleanse
> your hands, you sinners, and purify your hearts, you double-
> minded. Be wretched and mourn and weep. Let your laughter be
> turned to mourning and your joy to gloom. Humble yourselves before
> the Lord, and he will exalt you. (James 4:7–10)

This is the heart of formative discipline. We must bring our children back to the cross again and again. We must teach them why they sin, what the consequences are, and how Christ is their only hope.

REBUKE AND RESTRAIN THEM FROM EVERYTHING DETRIMENTAL TO THEIR SALVATION

Mather continues:

> I beseech you, parents, interpose your authority to stop and check
> the carriage of your children when they are running into the paths of
> the destroyer. Gratify them with rewards of well-doing when they do
> well, but do not let them gratify every ungodly vanity that their vain
> minds may be set upon. Keep a strict inspection upon their conver-
> sations; examine what company they keep; examine whether they
> take any bad course.[9]

This doesn't mean we can keep our children from sinning. Nevertheless, the fact that we cannot prevent sin must not keep us from restraining and rebuking it. A police officer doesn't watch a criminal commit a crime and refuse to act due to his inability to change a man's heart. No, he does what he can to resist the criminal and restrain him, knowing that his duty—while limited in its ultimate effectiveness—is necessary. It's the same for parents; though completely helpless when it comes to curing our children's sin, we must carry out our duty as far as it depends upon us.

Mather also writes:

> When your children do amiss, call them aside, set before them the precepts of God which they have broken, and the threatenings of God which they have provoked. Demand of them that they profess their sorrow for their faults, and that they resolve that they will be so faulty no more.[10]

We would do well to remember these four steps when our children transgress:

Call them aside. Take time to deal with the matter. Don't just fly off the handle or let it slide. Put down what you're doing and take your child aside. Let your child know that the matter is serious enough to merit your undivided attention.

Tell them what precept they've broken. Open your Bible and show your child why the Bible says what he did was wrong. Let him know that this isn't just a matter of preference, but one of absolute importance based on God's Word. If you can't find a precept in the Bible, ask yourself why you've deemed the behavior so heinous. It could be that you simply need to search further. However, you may be requiring more than God does.

Tell them what God threatens to those who so behave. Let your child know that God is serious about what they've done, and show them what his Word threatens for those who continue to do it. This may seem like manipulation, but it isn't. If God has warned us against something in his Word, we owe it to our children to point out the warning.

If our neighbor has a sign up that says "Beware of Dog," we certainly have no qualms about warning our children to stay off of his property. So why should we feel the slightest apprehension about telling them that God says, "But as for the cowardly, the faithless, the detestable, as for murderers, the sexually immoral, sorcerers, idolaters, and all liars, their portion will be in the lake that burns with fire and sulfur, which is the second death" (Rev. 21:8)? Is that not far more important than protecting your child from a neighbor's pet?

Call them to repent. Don't shy away from that word *repent,* or from what it represents. Our children must be called to acknowledge and forsake their sin. We must call them to repentance. Hear our Savior's words: "No, I tell you; but unless you repent, you will all likewise perish" (Luke 13:3). And again, "Repent, therefore, of this wickedness of yours, and pray to the Lord that, if possible, the intent of your heart may be forgiven you" (Acts 8:22).

LAY CHARGES UPON YOUR CHILDREN

Mather continues:

> Parents, charge them to work out their own salvation. . . . To charge them vehemently is to charm them wonderfully. Command your children, and it may be they will obey. Let God's commands be your commands, and it may be your children will obey them. Lay upon your children the charges of God.[11]

I didn't grow up with my father, nor was he a Christian for much of his life. However, I remember well the charges he gave me. I hope I never forget those things he said to me over and over again. There was wisdom in them, but there was also *him.* Those charges have outlived my father, so that although he now is dead, *he still speaks.*

It's important that we take advantage of every opportunity we have to lay a charge upon our children. Here are a few suggestions:

Charge your children with Scripture. While ol' folk wisdom is good (e.g., "a penny saved is a penny earned"), it's the Word of God that is "living and active, sharper than any two-edged sword, piercing to the division of soul and of spirit, of joints and of marrow, and discerning the thoughts and intentions of the heart" (Heb. 4:12). Do not settle for man's fallible sayings when you have God's infallible Word.

Charge your children before they fall. As noted earlier, it's important to rebuke our children when they sin. However, we must lay charge on them beforehand. We must press while the wax is hot and pliable. We must not leave our children with the impression that the Bible is only a tool for correction. "All Scripture is breathed out by God and profitable for teaching, for reproof, for correction, and for training in righteousness, that the man of God may be competent, equipped for every good work" (2 Tim. 3:16–17).

Charge your children repeatedly. If you have to tell them over and over again to brush their teeth, how much more will you have to remind them of these important precepts? Remember, "Faith comes from hearing, and hearing through the word of Christ" (Rom. 10:17). And again, "Therefore I intend always to remind you of these qualities, though you know them and are established in the truth that you have" (2 Pet. 1:12). We have a limited window of opportunity with our children, and there are myriad competing voices vying for their attention and allegiance. We must be diligent to charge them repeatedly with the things of God.

LIVE AN EXEMPLARY LIFE BEFORE YOUR CHILDREN

Reflect again on more of Mather's words:

> Your example may do much toward the salvation of your children; your works will more work upon your children than your words; your patterns will do more than your precepts, your copies more than your counsels.[12]

This is perhaps the most humbling principle Mather articulates. Which of us, if pressed on the matter, would not be forced to admit that much of the wickedness we so despise in our children is merely a reflection of the wickedness they've learned from us? This is precisely Mather's point when he adds these words:

> It will be impossible for you to infuse any good into your children if you appear void of that good yourselves. If the old crab goes backward, it is to no purpose for the young one to be directed to go forward. Sirs, young ones will crawl after the old ones.[13]

Elsewhere he asks, "Have you ungodly children? They may serve as a mirror, wherein you may behold something of your sinfulness before the Lord."[14] How true! How often have we failed to acknowledge our own sin and need for repentance as we demanded such from our children!

Another word for "formative discipline" is *discipleship*. In essence, we're teaching and modeling for our children. Hence, just as elders are "examples to the flock" (1 Pet. 5:3), family shepherds are examples to the family. When you tell your son to be kind to his siblings, do you do it with clenched teeth as you point a finger in his face? When you're at the end of your patience, and you tell your children to be quiet for the fifth time, are you doing so at the top of your voice?

This doesn't mean you cannot discipline your children until after you have everything squared away in your life. You can't wait for that because, first, you'll *never* get everything squared away in your life. Second, the way you handle your own sin and failings is part of what you're to model before your children. They need to see you fall on the sword when you've blown it. They need to hear heartfelt, unsolicited repentance from you. They have as their ultimate model one who lived a perfect life—and you're not that one. You merely point them to *him*.

PRAY FOR YOUR CHILDREN

Mather also writes,

> Pray for the salvation of your children, and carry the names of every one of them every day before the Lord with prayers, the cries whereof shall pierce the very heavens. Job 1:5: "He [Job] offered according to the number of all his children; thus Job did continually."[15]

This is the section in Mather's book where I usually lose it! No matter how much I pray for my children, I'm always reminded that it's not enough; it simply cannot be. I can say that I've prayed enough for my children only when each of their souls is secure with Christ.

Until then, I must follow this counsel:

> Wrestle with the Lord. Accept no denial. Earnestly protest, "Lord, I will not let Thee go unless Thou bless this poor child of mine and make him Thine own!" Do this until, if it may be, your heart is raised by a touch of heaven to a belief that God has blessed this child, who shall be blessed and saved forever.[16]

If we do nothing else, we must pray for our children. This is the heart of a true family shepherd; we cannot do this with sincerity and neglect to do all. For how can I pray for my children with this kind of fervor and neglect my plain duty? How can I love them enough to cry out to God on their behalf, but not love them enough to consider the condition of their souls, instruct them, rebuke them, lay charge upon them, and set an example for them?

Certainly this is the linchpin in formative discipline. Prayer will set my heart on all the matters mentioned above while reminding me that all of it is dependent upon the Lord and his mercy. Prayer will remind me that I'm in a spiritual battle with eternal consequences. And prayer will bend my will toward God and my heart toward my children.

Such prayer will also have an impact on our children directly, especially if we involve them in that prayer, as Mather counsels:

> O parents, why should you not now and then take one capable child after another alone before the Lord? Carry the child with you into your secret chambers; make the child kneel down by you while you present your children unto the Lord, and implore His blessing upon them. Let the child hear the groans and see the tears, and be a witness of the agonies wherein you are travailing for their salvation. The children will never forget what you do; it will have a marvelous force upon them.[17]

I hope you've come to see why I couldn't help but include Mather's words here. The Puritans had such a way with words, and their lives were so saturated with Scripture that their writings are among the most compelling things we can read.

Oh, that my own mind would be so saturated with God's truth!

Oh, that my parenting would reflect the passion for and dependence upon God that I sense in the writings of men like Cotton Mather!

And yet, how dare I expect anything less! After all, it is God who works in us both to will and to work for his good pleasure (Phil. 2:13)—and he's as real in our day as he was in Mather's.

CHAPTER TWELVE

CORRECTIVE DISCIPLINE

Listen to the Lord's words—spoken to the young boy and future prophet Samuel—concerning a certain leader of God's people who failed as a father:

> Behold, I am about to do a thing in Israel at which the two ears of everyone who hears it will tingle. On that day I will fulfill against Eli all that I have spoken concerning his house, from beginning to end. And I declare to him that I am about to punish his house forever, for the iniquity that he knew, because his sons were blaspheming God, and he did not restrain them. Therefore I swear to the house of Eli that the iniquity of Eli's house shall not be atoned for by sacrifice or offering forever. (1 Sam. 3:11–14)

I must admit that as a father I cannot read those words without trembling. I know it's in the Old Testament. I know that Eli and his sons were priests. I realize the unique nature of this prophecy. However, I cannot escape the underlying principle: Eli is being held accountable for failing to "restrain" his sons.

This parental duty is the same in the New Covenant as in the Old. Family shepherds are responsible for restraining the sin in their children.

As we begin exploring this, allow me to clarify. Eli is not being held accountable for his sons' being sinners. The Lord doesn't expect fathers to keep their children from all sin, but only that we *restrain* them.

Jonathan Edwards addressed this issue during the First Great Awakening:

> If you say you cannot restrain your children, this is no excuse; for it is a sign that you have brought up your children without govern-

ment, that your children regard not your authority. When parents lose their government over their children, their reproofs and counsel signify but little. How many parents are there who are exceedingly faulty on this account! How few are there who are thorough in maintaining order and government in their families! How is family-government in a great measure vanished! and how many are as likely to bring a curse upon their families, as Eli![1]

An illustration I used in the previous chapter is worth recalling and amplifying. Think of a woman being mugged on the street by a young thug as a policeman looks on. As you approach the officer to ask why he stood there and did nothing, would you be satisfied if he simply shrugged his shoulders, pointed to the young man running from the scene, and said, "You know how they are at that age"? Would that work for you? I doubt it. This would satisfy you no more than if he said, "That fellow did that because he's a sinner, and I could never change a sinner's heart." We don't ask police officers to change hearts, but to *restrain* evildoers! And that's precisely what parents are charged to do.

We cannot change our children's hearts any more than Eli could change the hearts of his sons. However we do, as Eli did, have a duty to restrain our children. That's where corrective discipline comes in. Family shepherds do not engage in corrective discipline because we believe it's efficacious for our children's salvation; we do so because it's a tool God has given us, and he expects us to employ it in the monumental task of bringing up our children "in the discipline and instruction of the Lord" (Eph. 6:4).

ASSUMPTIONS ASSOCIATED WITH CORRECTIVE DISCIPLINE

Parents who practice corrective discipline do so based on certain assumptions. It's these assumptions that shape the form of corrective discipline we employ.

Several assumptions must be in place if family shepherds are to lead their families in the area of biblical correction. Among other things, these assumptions concern biblical authority, absolutes, parental authority, and God's faithfulness.

BIBLICAL AUTHORITY

Corrective discipline assumes biblical authority. This ought to go without saying. However, many in our day question the authority, authenticity, and relevance of the Bible in virtually everything. As such, many Christians have a hard time knowing whether they can trust the Bible, and if so, how much or what parts?

This is especially true in the arena of corrective discipline, where professionals in fields such as education, psychology, child development, and social services are all singing from the same sheet of music and denouncing the Bible's chief form of corrective discipline, corporal punishment. Although as late as 1992 researchers noted that "most family physicians and pediatricians support the use of corporal punishment," and "most family physicians and pediatricians agree that children should be spanked if they misbehave," today's a different day.[2] Today the tables have turned. Thus the family shepherd must view the Bible as more authoritative than the cultural trend.

ABSOLUTES

Corrective discipline must also assume that there are absolutes. A family shepherd who doesn't believe that certain things are right and certain things are wrong, or who holds to a form of situational ethics, will not be committed to corrective discipline. And if he does correct his children, he'll do so inconsistently, as his subjective sense of right and wrong will be in constant flux.

Of course the absolutes upon which we build our corrective discipline are those we find in God's authoritative Word. It's not enough to believe that absolutes exist; we must also believe that God is the source of these ultimate truths. We cannot rely on ourselves, our culture, our education, or our family traditions.

PARENTAL AUTHORITY

Corrective discipline assumes the existence and appropriateness of parental authority. In our child-directed, anti-authoritarian, let-them-discover-who-they-are society, parental authority is increasingly considered a bad concept. It's a trend the family shepherd must be sensitive to and constantly oppose.

GOD'S FAITHFULNESS

Corrective discipline assumes that God is faithful and will fulfill all that he has promised. This is vitally important, because correcting children can be a frustrating endeavor. We don't simply confront our child's sin, correct them, and then be done with it. On the contrary, children have to be corrected repeatedly—multiple times a day, every day! Without a firm belief in God's faithfulness, we might "grow weary of doing good" (Gal. 6:9). We have to remind ourselves constantly that "whoever would draw near to God must believe that he exists and that he rewards those who seek him" (Heb. 11:6).

APPLICATION OF CORRECTIVE DISCIPLINE

Formative discipline, which we looked at in the previous chapter, is a family shepherd's most trusted and reliable tool. However, since our children are fallen creatures, they will most assuredly refuse to heed our admonitions at times, and will rebel against our authority. When that happens, formative discipline must give way to correction.

But what should that correction look like?

Paul Wegner has written an informative article in the *Journal of the Evangelical Theological Society* that outlines the increasing level of intensity in parental discipline prescribed in the book of Proverbs.[3] His outline is summarized here:

Level 1: Encourage proper behavior (e.g., Prov. 3:13–15; 4:7–8).
Level 2: Inform of improper behavior (Prov. 1:10–15; 3:31–32).
Level 3: Explain the negative consequences of sin (Prov. 1:18–19; 5:3–6).
Level 4: Gently exhort (Prov. 4:1–2; 14, 16).
Level 5: Gently rebuke or reprove (Prov. 3:12; 24:24–25).
Level 6: Apply corporal punishment that doesn't cause physical harm (Prov. 13:24; 19:18; 23:13–14; 29:15).

Level 7: Apply corporal punishment that causes physical harm (Prov. 10:31; 20:30). (On this topic, Wegner adds this: "The book of Proverbs does not suggest that parents use this technique for discipline, but that serious sin can lead to serious punishment. In a moral society sin can lead to destruction and sometimes warrants drastic punishment to curb the sinful behavior. In our society, we have given government, not parents, power to punish certain destructive behaviors. Even in Israel, judges and kings were given authority to deal with similar extreme behaviors."[4])

Level 8: Death.

Since levels one through four cover formative discipline (which we discussed in the previous chapter), and steps seven and eight cover extreme cases involving the civil magistrate, we'll focus our attention in this chapter on levels five and six. We examine the family shepherd's application of rebuke (or reproof) and of corporal punishment in the lives of his children.

REBUKE (REPROVE)

Reproof is an important tool for a family shepherd to have in his arsenal. There are times when other corrective discipline is impractical or impossible. For instance, you may be in a grocery store or other public place where it's inadvisable to use corporal punishment. Or you may be dealing with a child who has grown too old to spank (you know—like twenty or twenty-one).[5] Or you may be angry (in which case you should never spank a child). In those times, it's important to be able to *reprove* a child effectively.

But what exactly is reproof? In the Old Testament, the Hebrew word (*yākach*), which we translate as *rebuke*, can mean "dispute, reason together, prove; argue, judge, rule, reprove, rebuke; dispute (legally)."[6] Essentially, to reprove or rebuke means "to correct, to convince or convict" and "would not only imply exposure of one's sin but also to call a person to repentance."[7] In other words, we stop our children in their tracks, point out their sin and its consequences, and call them to repent.

There are a few things we must keep in mind as we do this.

REBUKE LOVINGLY

The word *rebuke* is often associated with harshness or a lack of gentleness. However, the word doesn't necessarily connote anger, rage, or bitterness. And it doesn't negate the command to "be angry and do not sin; do not let the sun go down on your anger, and give no opportunity to the devil" (Eph. 4:26–27). Reproof is done in love, not anger (Rev. 3:19).

Loving reproof is gentle. Pointing out sin in others is never to be done in arrogance. After all, we're as sinful as they are, and could even be sinning in the same way (see Matt. 7:1–5). A family shepherd must keep in mind his own sin—and the price Christ paid to redeem him from it—if he's to reprove his child gently.

Loving reproof is private whenever possible. The goal of rebuke is not humiliation, but correction. We should therefore always seek to reprove our children in private whenever possible. This can even be done in a crowded room if a parent masters the infamous "daddy stare." However, we must not lay this down as a rule in all cases, since public sin sometimes requires public rebuke.

Loving reproof seeks the child's best, not the parent's convenience. I like the term "family shepherd" for a number of reasons, including that it reminds me of the goal of my work. I'm shepherding my children toward Christ. My goal is not to raise children who conform to my hopes, wishes, dreams, or standards; my goal is to raise children who walk in the "discipline and instruction *of the Lord*" (Eph. 6:4). Hence, my reproof must always be geared toward leading them Christward.

REBUKE SPARINGLY

Rebuke means little without a pattern of kind, edifying words. It will signify little when I rebuke my child for his outright rebellion if I'm constantly rebuking him for every little thing he does.

The lion's share of our time should be spent on formative discipline, not forms of correction. We must *train* our children. Just like an athlete training for a big game, our children need multiple repetitions in order to master their discipline.

We can no more tell our children something one time and then expect to see their mastery in it than a basketball coach can explain how to shoot a jump shot and then immediately expect to see a player's perfect form. If a family shepherd finds himself constantly rebuking a child, he *could* be dealing with a significantly strong-willed, rebellious child. However, the more likely answer is that he has spent too little time training and too much time rebuking.

REBUKE THE SIN, NOT THE CHILD

Remember, your child has a disease; she's a sinner. It's the same disease with which *you* were born, and from which you await your ultimate deliverance.

Your child is not a uniquely sinful person, so don't treat her like she is. Rebuke the sin because it is sin and displeases God; don't rebuke the child because she has displeased her parent.

Also, we must heed Paul's admonition: "Let no corrupting talk come out of your mouths, but only such as is good for building up, as fits the occasion, that it may give grace to those who hear" (Eph. 4:29). This applies as continuously in the parent-child relationship as it does in any other.

CORPORAL PUNISHMENT

While there's a place for rebuke, it's not the last line of correction and must not be used as such. The ultimate level of parental correction is corporal punishment, or spanking. When a child has decided to rebel against parental authority, spanking is the authoritative response that reminds the child that the parent, under God, has the final word. However, this is by no means a license to abuse a child. "While the biblical text encourages the use of corporal punishment in the training of children, in the spirit of the wisdom of Proverbs it is prudent that the parent administer this discipline very carefully."[8]

FAMILY SHEPHERDS MUST SEE SPANKING AS BIBLICAL

"Folly is bound up in the heart of a child, but the rod of discipline drives it far from him" (Prov. 22:15). Ask a person over fifty what this verse means, and they'll probably answer in a statement like this: "It clearly means we ought to spank our children." They may also add, "And I wish some of these young parents would take it to heart." However, ask someone under forty, and you'll probably get quite a different response.

Younger parents have been influenced by secular, psychological thinking more than most of us know or care to admit. As a result, there are many Christian parents who read a verse like Proverbs 22:15 and have serious apprehensions. Immediately they question (1) whether the verse is to be taken literally, (2) whether such a practice is loving (since love is the *only* law they acknowledge), and (3) whether it's ever necessary. But an honest recognition of the Bible's authority removes those doubts.

FAMILY SHEPHERDS MUST SEE SPANKING AS LITERAL

In the *Good News Bible,* Proverbs 22:15 is paraphrased this way: "Children just naturally do silly, careless things, but a good spanking will teach them how to behave" (GNT). I rarely quote this particular Bible version, but they certainly got this one right (at least the second half of the verse). Even *The Message* uses the term "spanking" in its paraphrase of Proverbs 23:13. Yet, I still find myself having to constantly explain that spanking is the clear teaching of Scripture.

In some places in Scripture the idea of reproof or correction is obviously figurative. For example, when John records Jesus's words, "Those whom I love, I reprove and discipline, so be zealous and repent" (Rev. 3:19), it's obvious he doesn't mean to convey by that word "reprove" that God literally spanks his children. This is also the case when we read, "My son, do not despise the LORD's discipline or be weary of his reproof, for the LORD reproves him whom he loves, as a father the son in whom he delights" (Prov. 3:11–12). But in both cases, it would make absolutely no sense to use a metaphor for a practice that's metaphorical. It only makes sense that the Lord's discipline of his people would be an allusion to a heavenly reality that mirrors an earthly one.

This is clearly the case in many passages in Proverbs, as when we read, "On the lips of him who has understanding, wisdom is found, but a rod is for the back of him who lacks sense" (Prov. 10:13; see also 14:3; 26:3). Obviously the "rod" in question here is not metaphorical. This point is even clearer in Proverbs 23:13–14: "Do not withhold discipline from a child; if you strike him with a rod, he will not die. If you strike him with the rod, you will save his soul from Sheol." There's simply no way to read these verses in their normal sense and come away with the idea that the "rod" is somehow metaphorical.

WE MUST HELP FAMILY SHEPHERDS SEE THAT SPANKING IS LOVING

One of the great ironies of modern liberalism is its rejection of the "Law of God" in favor of the "Law of Love." The irony, of course, is that loving God and loving people is in fact the summary of the whole Law (Matt. 22:37–39; see also Lev. 19:18; Deut. 6:5). We must reject the false dichotomy that attempts to make enemies of these two friends. Moreover, we must recognize that love is not the absence of disapproval. There's more to love than mere acceptance and affection.

According to the Scriptures, "Whoever spares the rod hates his son, but he who loves him is diligent to discipline him" (Prov. 13:24). Though this may seem counterintuitive, we must recognize its deeper consistency and truth.

FAMILY SHEPHERDS MUST SEE SPANKING AS NECESSARY

Our culture throws out plenty of opposition to corporal punishment, sometimes in vehement protests—but they're not at all unique or even new. John Wesley faced (and refuted) similar arguments in his day. In his sermon on family religion, he observed, "Some will tell you, 'All this is lost labor: A child need not be corrected at all. Instruction, persuasion, and advice will be sufficient for any child without correction; especially if gentle reproof be added, as occasion may require.'"[9] Amazing how familiar that sounds! Wesley could have been quoting many a parenting book or newspaper advice column of today. And Wesley's response is just as appropriate now as it was then:

> I answer, "There may be particular instances, wherein this method may be successful. But you must not, in anywise, lay this down as an universal rule; unless you suppose yourself wiser than Solomon, or, to speak more properly wiser than God. For it is God himself, who best knoweth his own creatures, that has told us expressly, "He that spareth the rod, hateth his son: But he that loveth him chasteneth him betimes" (Proverbs 13:24). And upon this is grounded that plain commandment, directed to all that fear God, "Chasten thy son while there is hope, and let not thy soul spare for his crying" (Proverbs 19:18).[10]

Opposition to physical punishment isn't limited to "secular" detractors. Many say they oppose corporal discipline on "biblical" grounds. So parents today face pressure from without as well as within the camp. As a result, family shepherds will be hard-pressed to give answers to those who would use the very Bible that teaches spanking to oppose the practice.

For example, in an article in *Interpretation: A Journal of Bible and Theology,* Randall Heskett offers the following rationale:

> If one chooses to read the text literalistically, he or she must realize that Proverbs 23:13 states, "Do not withhold discipline from your son . . . " (author's translation) but it never mentions daughters. Therefore such literalism can only claim this form of punishment for sons but must at least spare daughters from the pain of spanking.[11]

While such folly is exposed quite easily by any thinking Christian with access to a Hebrew/English lexicon, it also falls victim to the use of translations other than Heskett's own. The Hebrew word he translates as "son" in the phrase "Do not withhold discipline from your son" is translated as "child" in the ESV, NIV, NKJV, NASB, KJV, RSV, ASV, and others. This is due to what should be the obvious nature of the Hebrew noun in question; it simply cannot be restricted to male children only.

The obvious question here is, why such folly? Why is Heskett, like many other critical "scholars," willing to go to such lengths to misconstrue the clear teaching of the text? He offers evidence of his philosophical presuppositions later when he writes:

> We need to read [biblical teaching on spanking] under the scrutiny of cross-cultural dialogue and interdisciplinary study. These proverbs, many of which were written over 3,000 years ago, are not static. They are not dead but alive. Their meaning and application change as humanity changes within the dynamic relationship of which wisdom functions as a middle discourse.[12]

The problem is therefore not so much what the text says, but what Heskett believes about the Bible in general. For him, because the text isn't "dead but alive," the Bible's meaning depends not on the author's intention but on the disposition of the reader.

This kind of folly is what family shepherds must see through, if we're going to promote biblical discipline. Arguments like Heskett's may sound convincing—especially when they appear in official-sounding publications like *Interpretation*—but they ultimately disown the authority of the Lord and his Word.

FAMILY SHEPHERDS MUST SEE SPANKING AS PART OF A BIGGER PICTURE

I chose to place this chapter at the end of the section on training and disciplining children for a reason. Corrective discipline is not an end in itself. We must understand it in the context of formative discipline and the overall discipleship of our children. We don't spank our children believing that corporal punishment is the last word, the end of the matter. We must understand that this is one of many tools in the toolbox.

And it's important to realize how much the culture in which we live has taken issue with this particular tool; we must be aware of its arguments and have answers to them. We must be convinced, ourselves, that this is God's way. We must believe what God has said, or we'll have no alternative but to forsake his ways and follow the spirit of the age—which is, of course, an untenable position.

We must obey God. The apostle Paul summed it up well: "Let God be true though every one were a liar, as it is written, 'That you may be justified in your words, and prevail when you are judged'" (Rom. 3:4).

A family shepherd would never abuse his children. Nor would he neglect to correct them in a manner commensurate with the teaching of God's Word. Balance in this matter can be a challenge, but the one who calls and commands us also equips us. God hasn't left us to figure this one out on our own. We have his word on the matter, and his word is more than trustworthy. It's the very standard by which all other claims to truth are judged.

PART FIVE

LIFESTYLE EVALUATION

EQUIPPING MEN TO COUNT THE COST OF FAMILY DISCIPLESHIP

CHAPTER THIRTEEN

CHURCH MEMBERSHIP

Church membership is *the* most important aspect of lifestyle evaluation.

Let that statement sink in for a minute. I'm arguing that *the* most important thing for a family shepherd to do—when he's evaluating how he's leading his family—is to ensure they're healthy members of a healthy church. This is more important than his assessment of their financial status, their use of time, their perspective on entertainment, where and how they live, what they drive, where and how their children are educated, or any other lifestyle issue. None of those things is as significant as church membership.

Now I realize that if you've lived and attended church in the United States of America for more than the last month, you may be convinced that I've just taken leave of my senses. You know that church membership is treated like a cheap commodity in our culture. In fact, you may have just left a church because you didn't like the music, or the carpet color, or the preacher, and you didn't even bother to tell them you were leaving. Moreover, they didn't even bother to notice (as is evidenced by the pledge cards for the new building campaign that you continue to receive in the mail).

Mark Dever captures the essence of this modern attitude toward the church in a brief chapter he wrote on church membership in 2001. He writes:

> Let's begin by admitting that the whole idea of church membership seems counter-productive to many today. Isn't it unfriendly, and maybe even elitist to say that some are in and others out? Can we go so far as to say that it is even unbiblical, and maybe even un-Christian? The end of Acts 2 simply says that "the Lord added to their

number" (that is, to the church) those who were being saved. Isn't that all there is to it? Also, in Acts 8, an official of the Ethiopian government had been traveling in Palestine and was returning home on his chariot, reading the prophet Isaiah. Philip was led by the Holy Spirit to intercept him and talk to him; the man believed and was baptized. In that case, wasn't the Ethiopian automatically a member of the church?[1]

Who among us hasn't thought, at one time or another, that the whole scenario of church involvement and commitment gets way overblown? But you may want to take a deep breath and listen to Dever's reprise:

> All of this is more important than many people today think it is. In fact, I'm convinced that getting this right is a key step toward revitalizing our churches, evangelizing our nation, furthering the cause of Christ around the world, and so bringing glory to God![2]

WHY MEMBERSHIP MATTERS

While Dever and others have done a wonderful job of providing clear, convincing arguments for church membership, the purpose of this chapter is to focus especially on the emphasis we place on church membership in equipping family shepherds. From that perspective, membership in the local church is indispensible for a number of reasons. Four of the most important to consider are *identification, edification, cooperation*, and *accountability*.

IDENTIFICATION WITH CHRIST AND THE CHURCH

It's important for family shepherds to see that their families are members of local churches so that they might be identified with Christ and his people.

Jesus himself identified this as one of the principle marks of genuine discipleship:

> A new commandment I give to you, that you love one another: just as I have loved you, you also are to love one another. By this all people will know that you are my disciples, if you have love for one another. (John 13:34–35)

One of the principle ways we demonstrate this "love for one another" is through membership in the local church. By sharing life together in identifiable communities, we exemplify Christian love as we celebrate together, labor together, and even suffer together.

This identification is also important from a doctrinal perspective. For instance, a person who professes to believe in Christ but actually holds to Mormon doctrine is easily identified by his or her membership in a Mormon body. By the same token, those who are members in good standing of healthy, theologically sound local bodies bear witness to the truths their church upholds. In fact, drawing such distinctions is one of the primary functions of church leaders (see Titus 1:9). Again, Mark Dever's words on this are spot on:

> God intends us to be together in this way to expose false gospels. It is through our coming together as Christians that we show the world what Christianity really is. In our churches, we debunk messages and images which purport to be biblical Christianity but really are not. Must it not surely be the case that some of those who are not members of evangelical churches are not so because they do not really believe the same evangel? Part of the church's mission is to recognize and defend the true gospel and to prevent perversions of it.[3]

Thus, we must recognize the importance of identification with the local church not only for ourselves, but also for the sake of the gospel. The people of God gather together and bear witness to the truth while simultaneously exposing falsehood. This ought to be the goal of every believer. Moreover, it ought to be a legacy every father desires to pass on to his children.

Far too often parents take church membership lightly, only to see their children do the same when they leave the home. Only then the parents begin to complain: "Oh, how I wish Johnny would take his family to church."

EDIFICATION

While identification with Christ and his church is important, it's not nearly enough. Church membership also serves as a means of edification.

Three centuries ago, the Second London Baptist Confession affirmed the Lord's mandate to us concerning the church in these words:

> In the execution of this power wherewith he is so entrusted, the Lord Jesus calls out of the world unto himself, through the ministry of his word, by his Spirit, those that are given unto him by his Father, that they may walk before him in all the ways of obedience, which he prescribes to them in his word. Those thus called, he commands to walk together in particular societies, or churches, for their mutual edification, and the due performance of that public worship, which he requires of them in the world.[4]

The family shepherd who neglects to encourage his family toward healthy church membership is actually robbing them of a great blessing. He's keeping them from those ordinary means of grace that are essential to the health, growth, and well-being of every believer.

The apostle Paul paints a vivid picture of the mutual edification that accompanies healthy church membership in his epistle to the Colossian Christians:

> Put on then, as God's chosen ones, holy and beloved, compassionate hearts, kindness, humility, meekness, and patience, bearing with one another and, if one has a complaint against another, forgiving each other; as the Lord has forgiven you, so you also must forgive. And above all these put on love, which binds everything together in perfect harmony. And let the peace of Christ rule in your hearts, to which indeed you were called in one body. And be thankful. Let the word of Christ dwell in you richly, teaching and admonishing one another in all wisdom, singing psalms and hymns and spiritual songs, with thankfulness in your hearts to God. (Col. 3:12–16)

While Christians should express these character qualities and accompanying attitudes regardless of their context, this passage could neither be reduced to the work of the individual family nor limited to the universal church. This is a picture of unity and edification within the context of *a worshiping body of believers*.

Paul's words in Ephesians are even more poignant, as he

alludes to the function of the officers of the church as means of edification:

> And he gave the apostles, the prophets, the evangelists, the shepherds and teachers, to equip the saints for the work of ministry, for building up the body of Christ, until we all attain to the unity of the faith and of the knowledge of the Son of God, to mature manhood, to the measure of the stature of the fullness of Christ, so that we may no longer be children, tossed to and fro by the waves and carried about by every wind of doctrine, by human cunning, by craftiness in deceitful schemes. Rather, speaking the truth in love, we are to grow up in every way into him who is the head, into Christ, from whom the whole body, joined and held together by every joint with which it is equipped, when each part is working properly, makes the body grow so that it builds itself up in love. (Eph. 4:11–16)

Here we see the roles of local church officers highlighted in the context of Christ's work of sanctification. Thus, local church membership is a means of edification that no family shepherd should neglect personally, or fail to press home to his family.

COOPERATION

Of course, there's more to church membership than the benefits that accrue to the member. There's also the benefit to the mission of the church as a whole. As we join together in local bodies, we can accomplish more through our cooperation than any of us could accomplish alone. This is true in both evangelism (Matt. 28:16–20) and in ministries of mercy. A family shepherd with a vision for ministry can have a tremendous impact in and through his family (as well he should). However, the synergy that's created when a group of like-minded families who are being shepherded in this way come together can be awe-inspiring.

While few Christians need convincing when it comes to our call to cooperate in the matter of evangelism, most are either unaware or misinformed when it comes to the role of the church in ministries of mercy. On the one end of the spectrum are those who view any and all mercy ministry as "social gospel"; those on the other end of the spectrum view the church as nothing more than the Red Cross with weekly sermons. Somewhere in the middle is the biblical mandate.

One clear example of this is in Paul's first letter to Timothy. Here, Paul outlines the church's obligation as it relates to widows. As he does so, he demonstrates the beautiful synergy between the ministry of the church and the responsibilities of the home: "If any believing woman has relatives who are widows, let her care for them. Let the church not be burdened, so that it may care for those who are truly widows" (1 Tim. 5:16). Thus, equipping family shepherds must include clear instruction about the jurisdictions and responsibilities of these two institutions—family and church—and the beauty and necessity of their cooperation.

There's an unfortunate tendency among some fathers who grasp the magnitude of their responsibilities in discipling their families to overcorrect when it comes to the question of biblical jurisdictions. As a result, they expend much time, energy, effort, and resources in attempting to do alone what God has called us to do together in the church.

Such cooperation is a wonderful benefit of healthy church membership, and those of us committed to equipping family shepherds must communicate this benefit clearly and consistently.

ACCOUNTABILITY

Perhaps the most difficult benefit of church membership to communicate is accountability. Despite that difficulty, accountability serves as a crucial element of healthy church membership that serious family shepherds should embrace.

We all need accountability. The Bible is replete with examples of the kind of healthy accountability the church is designed to provide. For instance, Jesus teaches that the church serves as the final authority in matters of discipline involving members:

> If your brother sins against you, go and tell him his fault, between you and him alone. If he listens to you, you have gained your brother. But if he does not listen, take one or two others along with you,

that every charge may be established by the evidence of two or three witnesses. If he refuses to listen to them, tell it to the church. And if he refuses to listen even to the church, let him be to you as a Gentile and a tax collector. (Matt. 18:15–17)

This kind of accountability would be meaningless without a local church having clear boundaries and expectations regarding membership.

A specific example of this kind of accountability is found in Paul's first letter to the church in Corinth:

It is actually reported that there is sexual immorality among you, and of a kind that is not tolerated even among pagans, for a man has his father's wife. And you are arrogant! Ought you not rather to mourn? Let him who has done this be removed from among you.

For though absent in body, I am present in spirit; and as if present, I have already pronounced judgment on the one who did such a thing. When you are assembled in the name of the Lord Jesus and my spirit is present, with the power of our Lord Jesus, you are to deliver this man to Satan for the destruction of the flesh, so that his spirit may be saved in the day of the Lord. (1 Cor. 5:1–5)

Paul goes on to write, "God judges those outside. 'Purge the evil person from among you'" (1 Cor. 5:13). Again, there's a clear distinction between those "inside" and "outside" the specific body.

WHY MEMBERSHIP MATTERS MORE THAN OTHER LIFESTYLE EVALUATION ISSUES

In this final section of the book on lifestyle evaluation, we begin with church membership because there's no other issue more crucial in this area. Healthy membership in a healthy church is the foundation upon which the rest of our lifestyle evaluation is built. A healthy church will expose us to the regular teaching, preaching, reading, and singing of the Word of God that will shape the way we think about all other aspects of life. Genuine relationships with other believers will help bring us balance as we share life together. Mature men and women in the church will gently call us out when we go off the deep end. Elders who are functioning biblically will get to know us and our families, becoming familiar with our strengths, weaknesses, hopes, dreams, and needs.

In the next two chapters, as we contemplate how we spend our time and money, it's important that we realize that being a healthy member of a healthy church will have a direct impact on those issues as well. Let me make the simple statement again: There's *nothing* we can do for our families that will have a greater positive impact than making sure we're healthy members of a healthy local church.

I've seen evidence of this firsthand as I've had conversation after conversation with fathers and mothers who are committed to family discipleship, but who are struggling tremendously as they either attend an unhealthy church or no church at all. These families don't testify of overwhelming joy and fulfillment because "family is enough." On the contrary, they testify to struggle, strain, loneliness, fear, isolation, and despair.

Family discipleship is absolutely crucial, but there's no substitute for healthy membership in a healthy local church.

CHAPTER FOURTEEN

OUR USE OF TIME

The use of time is one of the most difficult subjects to broach with Christian men. We've grown so accustomed to burning the candle at both ends that we tend to bristle at any suggestion that we need to "dial it back" a bit to make time for that which matters most. Nevertheless, we cannot equip family shepherds effectively without addressing the issue of our schedules.

Paul writes, "Look carefully then how you walk, not as unwise but as wise, making the best use of the time, because the days are evil" (Eph. 5:15–16). These words from the apostle often go unnoticed, or at least unheeded. Rare indeed is the man who looks honestly at his use of time in light of eternity. And yet, that's precisely what we must do.

My goal here is not to give an exhaustive treatment of time management. Instead, I wish to draw attention to several overarching principles that, if understood, will lay the groundwork necessary for an honest evaluation of our time, as well as a grid for our reform and improvement in this area.

THE FOURTH COMMANDMENT AND THE PACE OF LIFE

Why do we have such a thing as "a week"?

Think about what a unique concept the week actually is. Days, months, and years are all related to the earth's relationship to the sun and moon. Once around the earth's axis is a day. One orbit of the moon around the earth is a month. And one orbit of the earth around the sun is a year. Very simple. However, there are no heavenly bodies that mark off a week. The only thing in the history of the world that explains the existence of the very concept of the week is the creation account at the beginning of the book of Genesis.

God established the concept of the week when he created the world—and in doing so, he established a barometer for our pace of life:

> Thus the heavens and the earth were finished, and all the host of them. And on the seventh day God finished his work that he had done, and he rested on the seventh day from all his work that he had done. So God blessed the seventh day and made it holy, because on it God rested from all his work that he had done in creation. (Gen. 2:1–3)

So the pattern is a seven-day week—six for work and one for rest.

God reemphasizes this point when he gives Moses the Ten Commandments:

> Remember the Sabbath day, to keep it holy. Six days you shall labor, and do all your work, but the seventh day is a Sabbath *to the* LORD your God. On it you shall not do any work, you, or your son, or your daughter, your male servant, or your female servant, or your livestock, or the sojourner who is within your gates. For in six days the LORD made heaven and earth, the sea, and all that is in them, and rested on the seventh day. Therefore the LORD blessed the Sabbath day and made it holy. (Ex. 20:8–11)

Here God puts an even finer point on the matter. Now we see not only that there are six days for work and one for rest, but also that there are six days for our affairs and one for God's. This concept is carried straight through the New Testament, and remains true today as evidenced by our worship on the Lord's Day (Sunday, the day of Christ's resurrection).

CAN YOU GIVE GOD A DAY?

As a result of the biblical foundation, family shepherds have an obligation not only to "take a day off" but also to serve God on that day. B. B. Warfield explains:

[T]he Sabbath, in our Lord's view, was not a day of sheer idleness; inactivity was not its mark. Inactivity was not the mark of God's Sabbath, when he rested from the works, which he creatively made. Up to this very moment he has been working continuously; and, imitating him, our Sabbath is also to be filled with work. In one word, the Sabbath is the Lord's Day, not ours; and on it is to be done the Lord's work, not ours; and that is our "rest."[1]

Warfield's assessment is not unique. Thomas Boston referred to the Sabbath as "a rest without a rest, wherein the soul is most busy and active, serving the Lord without weariness."[2]

For most Christians in our culture, the idea of a Christian Sabbath is completely foreign. Read, for example, the words of Thomas Boston, and try to picture them coming from the pulpit of an American megachurch:

The Sabbath day is not capable of any sanctity or holiness, but what is relative; that is, in respect of its use for holy rest or exercise. So, (1) God has sanctified that day, by setting it apart for holy uses, designing and appointing it in a special manner for his own worship and service. (2) Men must sanctify it by keeping it holy, spending that day in God's worship and service for which God has set it apart; using it only for the uses that God has consecrated it unto.[3]

Chances are, unless you've been running in certain conservative Presbyterian or Reformed Baptist circles, you've never heard such a position espoused, let alone seen the types of extremes to which some have carried the idea, as John Owen notes in his commentary on Hebrews:

Others again have collected whatever they could think of, that is good, pious, and useful in the practice of religion, and prescribed it all in a multitude of instances, as necessary to the sanctification of this day; so that a man can scarcely in six days read over all the duties that are proposed to be observed on the seventh.[4]

My goal is not to convince you to adopt Boston's position. And I certainly wouldn't recommend carrying the idea as far as those to whom Owen is referring take it. However, I do want you to consider the way you spend the Lord's Day and whether it honors God. Does your life reflect the pattern God built into creation? Do you give sufficient attention to the day Jesus set apart by his resurrection from the dead (Mark 16:2, 9; Luke 24:1; John 20:1)? Or do you treat the Lord's Day like those whom Amos condemns:

> Hear this, you who trample on the needy
> and bring the poor of the land to an end,
> saying, "When will the new moon be over,
> that we may sell grain?
> And the Sabbath,
> that we may offer wheat for sale,
> that we may make the ephah small and the shekel great
> and deal deceitfully with false balances,
> that we may buy the poor for silver
> and the needy for a pair of sandals
> and sell the chaff of the wheat?"
>
> The Lord has sworn by the pride of Jacob:
> "Surely I will never forget any of their deeds.
> Shall not the land tremble on this account,
> and everyone mourn who dwells in it,
> and all of it rise like the Nile,
> and be tossed about and sink again, like the Nile of Egypt?" (Amos 8:4–8)

CAN YOU GIVE GOD YOUR WORK WEEK?

Amos brings up a point that must not be overlooked. One of the dangers we face when we talk to men about the idea of the Sabbath and the Lord's Day is that we may give a false impression that only one day in seven belongs to God. We must be sure to help family shepherds realize that the Sabbath has to do with the *pace of life*; it doesn't negate God's sovereignty over everything else. If we're going to work six days a week in a job that's an abomination to God (one that, for example, causes us to "trample on the needy and bring the poor of the land to an end"), then showing up at church on the Lord's Day doesn't cut it.

An extreme example of this kind of thinking was evident in the life of Dr. George Tiller. Tiller was the late-term abortionist who was gunned down in 2009 at an unusual location—his church, where he was a member in good standing. One of Tiller's fellow parishioners was quoted as saying, "The church has stood back behind Dr. Tiller," while describing him as "a Christian, good man." This "good man" was one who by his own count had taken the lives of over sixty thousand unborn babies, most of them late-term. Such an example, while extreme, makes the point quite clearly. There's a sense in which George Tiller is a grotesque example of many men who see a complete separation between the way they make their living and the way they serve their God.

A family shepherd has a duty to model for his family and lead them in a manner that brings honor to the Lord. This must include the way he chooses to make a living. We must not forget Jesus's words:

> Therefore I tell you, do not be anxious about your life, what you will eat or what you will drink, nor about your body, what you will put on. Is not life more than food, and the body more than clothing? Look at the birds of the air: they neither sow nor reap nor gather into barns, and yet your heavenly Father feeds them. Are you not of more value than they? And which of you by being anxious can add a single hour to his span of life? And why are you anxious about clothing? Consider the lilies of the field, how they grow: they neither toil nor spin, yet I tell you, even Solomon in all his glory was not arrayed like one of these. But if God so clothes the grass of the field, which today is alive and tomorrow is thrown into the oven, will he not much more clothe you, O you of little faith? Therefore do not be anxious, saying, "What shall we eat?" or "What shall we drink?" or "What shall we wear?" For the Gentiles seek after all these things, and your heavenly Father knows that you need them all. (Matt. 6:25–32)

We mustn't live like those with "little faith" who compromise for the sake of food and clothing. What we do matters. And not every job is a good job.

Jesus completes his thought by pointing to the guiding principle in all of this: "Seek first the kingdom of God and his righteousness, and all these things will be added to you" (Matt. 6:33). We must believe that God will not forsake those who seek him.

As family shepherds, we have an obligation to lead our families in righteousness. The pursuit of ill-gotten gain sends the wrong message. It says that Monday through Saturday doesn't matter. It says that God is only concerned with what we do on the Lord's Day. Most importantly, it says that we don't trust the Lord to provide for us and meet our needs if we choose to seek righteousness.

CAN YOU GIVE GOD YOUR DOWN TIME?

Once the big picture is in focus, the family shepherd can see clearly how to address the "smaller" issues like entertainment, recreation, and leisure. And believe me when I say that a commitment to shepherding your family will bring these issues to the fore.

Bill is one example. Bill was an avid Texas football fan. He watched his boy's high school games on Friday nights, watched college games all day Saturday, and watched professional games on Sunday afternoon, Sunday night, and Monday night. He made sure to attend the annual Texas/Oklahoma and Texas/Texas A&M games (plus a bowl game if his team made it). Through his job, he also had access to season tickets for the Houston Texans in the NFL. In other words, from August to February, Bill wasn't much of a church member.

One day, Bill got serious about being a family shepherd. He started leading family worship regularly in his home. He took ownership of the discipleship of his sons, and he found a healthy local church that did more than stroke his ego and beg for his money. Bill also started learning about the idea of a biblical pace of life. No one told him his football consumption had to change. However, it didn't take a degree in rocket science for him to figure out that he couldn't continue his pace of entertainment consumption and be serious about shepherding his family and participating fully in his church.

Bill still loves football. And you'll probably still find him at the big Texas/OU game each fall. However, his former appetites have given way to more meaningful pursuits. What's more, he doesn't miss it like he thought he would—though the withdrawal was epic.

There's a Bill in all of us. Our entertainment-driven culture has provided us with laptops, iPods, iPads, iPhones, Droids, Wi-Fi, XM, TiVo, and a whole host of other devices and mechanisms to keep us plugged into the matrix. If we're not purposeful, the cultural inertia will make it impossible to live meaningful lives. We'll look up one day and our kids will be gone—and all we'll be able to say is, "I wish I'd taken better advantage of the time."

There's much to enjoy in this world, and we should enjoy it. However, none of it is as important as the privilege and obligation we have to "tell to the coming generation the glorious deeds of the LORD, and his might, and the wonders that he has done" (Ps. 78:4). A family shepherd must always keep this in mind.

CHAPTER FIFTEEN

DUAL CITIZENSHIP

There's much more that can be said concerning lifestyle evaluation. In fact, there's *too* much more. As I considered this last section, I realized that it could be an entire book in itself.

Calling family shepherds to consider the way they live is a daunting and endless task—but it must be done. We must recognize that we're citizens of two kingdoms—the kingdom of God and the kingdom of man. And one of those passports always trumps the other. As the apostle John wrote so poignantly,

> Do not love the world or the things in the world. If anyone loves the world, the love of the Father is not in him. For all that is in the world—the desires of the flesh and the desires of the eyes and pride in possessions—is not from the Father but is from the world. And the world is passing away along with its desires, but whoever does the will of God abides forever. (1 John 2:15–17)

The apostle James puts an even finer point on the matter when he writes, "Do you not know that friendship with the world is enmity with God? Therefore whoever wishes to be a friend of the world makes himself an enemy of God" (James 4:4).

Of course, both John and James are merely echoing the words of their Lord and teacher, Jesus. "If you were of the world," our Lord said, "the world would love you as its own; but because you are not of the world, but I chose you out of the world, therefore the world hates you" (John 15:19). This is, in fact, a consistent theme in John's Gospel.[1]

Although believers are not to love the world, and the world hates us, we're still called to be a part of that world: "I do not ask that you take them out of the world," Jesus prayed, "but that you keep them from the evil one" (John 17:15). Herein lies the difficult task of balancing our roles in two kingdoms. This isn't something that happens automatically. Nor is it a small matter. Family shepherds who fail to grasp this truth will be prone to fall into one of a number of errors, as Kim Riddlebarger observes:

> When these two kingdoms are confused or conflated, we see the rise of the "social gospel" of Protestant liberalism, American civil religion of the Christian right and the liberal left, as well as the rise of Constantianism (Christendom). The church must never take up the sword and Caesar must never enter the pulpit.[2]

We must remember several basic tenets as we consider how we as family shepherds lead our families to live as citizens of two kingdoms. Riddlebarger helpfully offers six principles we must keep in mind:

1. Christ is Lord of both kingdoms.
2. Every Christian is simultaneously a citizen of both kingdoms (Phil. 3:20; Rom. 13:1–7).
3. The state is a post-fall, common-grace institution given by God for the administration of justice and to restrain evil (Rom. 13:1–7).
4. Non-Christians do not accept or acknowledge Christ's Lordship over the civil kingdom. This is the basis for the antithesis between Christian and non-Christian ways of thinking and doing. The failure to acknowledge Christ's Lordship renders one guilty before God (Rom. 1:18–25), but does not invalidate the civil kingdom or the non-Christian's place in it.
5. While Paul calls Rome a minister of God (Rom. 13:4), a generation later John describes that same empire as the beast, empowered by the dragon to persecute the people of God (Revelation 13). The Christian's confession that "Jesus is Lord," is likewise a confession that Caesar isn't.
6. From the time Adam was cast from Eden, God has intended the kingdom of Christ (the church) to dwell and advance in the midst of the civil kingdom (the world). This is the foundation for the missionary endeavors of the church, as well as a hedge against either utopianism (an overrealized eschatology) or escapism (i.e., monasticism).[3]

These principles give us valuable help in learning to be kingdom-minded.

THE KINGDOM OF GOD

The "kingdom of God" can be defined in a number of ways. For our purposes, we can define the kingdom of God simply as his kingship, or his rule, or his authority.[4] While there's much that can be said about the nature and function of that kingdom, family shepherds need to know and apply at least two main truths as they lead their families to operate from a kingdom perspective.

First, we must view God's kingdom as distinct from the kingdom of the world. Second, we must view ourselves as ambassadors of the kingdom of God, heralding its message. And we do so as God himself expands his kingship, rule, and authority through calling men, women, boys, and girls out of darkness (the kingdom of this world) into his marvelous light (the kingdom of God).

A DISTINCT PEOPLE

As citizens of the kingdom of God we live in the world, yet the kingdom of God is distinct from that world. Peter captures this reality poetically in his first epistle:

> But you are a chosen race, a royal priesthood, a holy nation, a people for his own possession, that you may proclaim the excellencies of him who called you out of darkness into his marvelous light. Once you were not a people, but now you are God's people; once you had not received mercy, but now you have received mercy. (1 Pet. 2:9–10)

How different would our families look if we operated from this perspective? Think about the ways it would impact the many decisions we make. Would we think the same way about our careers, our neighbors, or the education of our children? Would we make the same decisions about the way we handle our money, spend our leisure time, or invest our talents? Of course there would be a difference! That's precisely why family shepherds must consider these truths.

This perspective also changes the way we think about the church. No longer will we be able to view it as a social club. A kingdom mentality lends itself to a more biblical perspective as we walk in unity with our brothers and sisters and exercise our gifts for the benefit of the body (Rom. 12:3–8; 1 Cor. 12:1–31).

OUR CALLING AS AMBASSADORS

If we view ourselves as citizens of the kingdom of God who enjoy all the rights and privileges therein, we must also recognize that the vast majority of people with whom we come in contact every day are citizens of the kingdom of this world—and therefore enemies of God (Rom. 11:28; 1 Cor. 15:25; Phil. 3:18; Heb. 1:13; 10:13) as well as objects of his wrath (Rom. 1:18; Eph. 2:3–4). We must have a heart that reflects Jesus's admonition to "pray earnestly to the Lord of the harvest to send out laborers into his harvest" (Matt. 9:38). Moreover, we must be willing to heed that call ourselves.

Every family shepherd ought at least to consider how he and his family can be involved in carrying out the church's Great Commission (Matt. 28:18–20). We must also keep in mind that God calls some men to serve in capacities that extend beyond their own families. Remember, "He gave the apostles, the prophets, the evangelists, the shepherds and teachers, to equip the saints for the work of ministry, for building up the body of Christ" (Eph. 4:11–12). And again, "If anyone aspires to the office of overseer, he desires a noble task" (1 Tim. 3:1).

This message of the kingdom is passed on from generation to generation through the ministry taking place in homes (as we've seen)—but we must also remember that the church is always God's Plan A. Therefore we must always be on the lookout for those faithful men who will be able to teach others that which the apostles have taught (2 Tim. 2:2). Paul explains why this is so crucial:

> How then will they call on him in whom they have not believed? And how are they to believe in him of whom they have never heard? And how are they to hear without someone preaching? And how are they

to preach unless they are sent? As it is written, "How beautiful are the feet of those who preach the good news!" (Rom. 10:14–15)

One of the benefits of raising up family shepherds is that the home (as we've discussed) is a training and proving ground for church leadership. As men teach the Scriptures, lead family worship, catechize, and disciple in their homes, God may indeed open their eyes to a broader calling.

THE KINGDOM OF MAN

Although we're citizens of the kingdom of God, we're residents in the kingdom of man, and we must be strategic about how we live therein. Peter aptly summarizes what this strategy should include:

> Be subject for the Lord's sake to every human institution, whether it be to the emperor as supreme, or to governors as sent by him to punish those who do evil and to praise those who do good. For this is the will of God, that by doing good you should put to silence the ignorance of foolish people. Live as people who are free, not using your freedom as a cover-up for evil, but living as servants of God. Honor everyone. Love the brotherhood. Fear God. Honor the emperor. (1 Pet. 2:13–17)

In light of this and other admonitions in Scripture, there are many areas where every family shepherd will have to apply these truths to the way they lead their families. Let's look at some of those areas—government, business, and economics.

GOVERNMENT

There's a clear connection to government in Peter's words quoted above. As Christians, we must recognize that God in his sovereignty has established the institution of government, and we as believers are commanded to submit to governmental authority (Rom. 13:1–4). But what does that mean? And how is a family shepherd to lead his family in this area?

Let me offer some suggestions.

Know your government. If family shepherds are to be effective influencers in the kingdom of man, they're going to have to know their government. That sounds obvious, but you would be surprised how many Christian men (1) don't understand the type of government under which they live, (2) don't know who rules or represents them, or (3) don't really care about any of this. At our church we pray for a different local, state, and national leader each week. One of our goals is to help people know their government.

Be your government. If you have the privilege of living in a constitutional representative republic like I do (no, America is not a "democracy" in the pure sense of the word), then there are opportunities—obligations, in fact—to which you must attend. These can include voting, petitioning, or even running for public office. Whatever the case, it takes involvement. Thus, it's crucial at the very least that we know the key political issues of our day and learn to think biblically about them. How else can we vote, petition, or lead effectively?

Challenge your government. This may sound like a contradiction in light of the biblical mandate to submit. However, submission to God always supersedes submission to anyone else. If and when the time comes, we must challenge our government; at the very least, we should point out reasons why we cannot comply with or support certain actions. This is precisely what Peter and John did before the Sanhedrin when they said, "Whether it is right in the sight of God to listen to you rather than to God, you must judge, for we cannot but speak of what we have seen and heard" (Acts 4:19–20).

BUSINESS AND ECONOMICS

Between 2004 and 2006, the world was focused on the Enron crisis. Ken Lay was a household name, quickly becoming a pejorative term. Nowhere was this truer than where I live—in Houston, Texas. In addition to the public ridicule and scorn, we had to deal with the economic fallout as scores of companies related to Enron, either directly or indirectly, tried to stay alive. Thousands of Houstonians lost their jobs or their retirement funds, and the business world got a black eye.

What was interesting to me, though, was to watch Ken Lay walk through the entire process with his pastor by his side. As I watched, I couldn't help but wonder if this prominent multimillionaire had ever been handed a book on business or economics by one of his shepherds. Had they ever told him, "A just balance and scales are the LORD's; all the weights in the bag are his work" (Prov. 16:11)? Had they mentioned the fact that "unequal weights are an abomination to the LORD, and false scales are not good" (Prov. 20:23)? Had they issued the prophet Micah's warning: "Shall I acquit the man with wicked scales and with a bag of deceitful weights?" (Mic. 6:11). Or did they merely prop Ken Lay up as a man of prominence because he was a multimillionaire and they were proud to have him on board?

I don't know the answers to those questions. However, I know it made me think about my obligation as a pastor. Forget the megachurch to which he belonged; would Mr. Lay have gotten those things from me?

We have to remember that family shepherds live and work in the kingdom of man, and as such they need to be equipped to be ambassadors. Thus, being a God-honoring employer or employee is as appropriate a topic of discussion as how to lead family worship.

GOD-HONORING EMPLOYEES

The apostle Paul has left us a clear example of the appropriateness of addressing men and their work:

> For you yourselves know how you ought to imitate us, because we were not idle when we were with you, nor did we eat anyone's bread without paying for it, but with toil and labor we worked night and day, that we might not be a burden to any of you. It was not because we do not have that right, but to give you in ourselves an example to imitate. For even when we were with you, we would give you this command: If anyone is not willing to work, let him not eat. For we hear that some among you walk in idleness, not busy at work, but busybodies. Now such persons we command and encourage in the Lord Jesus Christ to do their work quietly and to earn their own living. (2 Thess. 3:7–12)

Certainly Paul didn't consider the matter of how men engaged in commerce to be something beneath him. As such, it's also a matter worthy of our consideration.

The overwhelming majority of family shepherds are employees who work for someone other than themselves. This means they're obligated to give their employer an honest day's work for an honest day's pay. Moreover, as in all things, God's people should be marked by excellence: "Do you see a man skillful in his work? He will stand before kings; he will not stand before obscure men" (Prov. 22:29).

The Bible also makes it clear that our work is not to be done merely to please those who employ us; rather, "whatever you do, work heartily, as *for the Lord* and not for men" (Col. 3:23; see also Eccles. 9:10). And although the following words were directed to slaves, Paul's admonition in Ephesians 6 is clearly appropriate in today's work arena as well:

> Obey your earthly masters with fear and trembling, with a sincere heart, as you would Christ, not by the way of eye-service, as people-pleasers, but as servants of Christ, doing the will of God from the heart, rendering service with a good will as to the Lord and not to man, knowing that whatever good anyone does, this he will receive back from the Lord, whether he is a slave or free. (Eph. 6:5–8)

Elsewhere Paul exhorts slaves to be "well-pleasing, not argumentative, not pilfering, but showing all good faith, so that in everything they may adorn the doctrine of God our Savior" (Titus 2:9–10). Note that Paul's admonition was not limited to those with believing masters. This is clear because elsewhere he addresses the idea of serving a believing master as another issue altogether: "Those who have believing masters must not be disrespectful on the ground that they are brothers; rather they must serve all the better since those who benefit by their good service are believers and beloved" (1 Tim. 6:2).

If this applied to a slave, it most assuredly applies to one working for wages. Think about it: Paul required this of men who were the property of other men. How much more should we seek to glorify Christ in the way we work for others who compensate us for that labor.

GOD-HONORING EMPLOYERS

In addition to the precepts mentioned above, some men have to keep in mind other important guidelines, because they serve as employers. With greater influence comes greater responsibility. However, we're all still servants of God. Therefore Paul says, "Masters, treat your slaves justly and fairly, knowing that you also have a Master in heaven" (Col. 4:1). And again he urges, "Masters . . . stop your threatening, knowing that he who is both their Master and yours is in heaven, and that there is no partiality with him" (Eph. 6:9).

Here Paul comes to the ultimate point. Regardless of whether we're rich or poor, employer or employee, we're citizens of the kingdom of God, and our work in the kingdom of man is always to be done with that truth in mind. We must remember that while our livelihood may be tied up in the kingdom of man, our future is not:

> The end of all things is at hand; therefore be self-controlled and so-ber-minded for the sake of your prayers. Above all, keep loving one another earnestly, since love covers a multitude of sins. Show hospitality to one another without grumbling. As each has received a gift, use it to serve one another, as good stewards of God's varied grace: whoever speaks, as one who speaks oracles of God; whoever serves, as one who serves by the strength that God supplies—in order that in everything God may be glorified through Jesus Christ. To him belong glory and dominion forever and ever. Amen. (1 Pet. 4:7–11)

A SPECIAL CONCERN
WHAT ABOUT FATHERLESS FAMILIES?

Being a single mother is one of the toughest jobs in the world. God designed the family in such a way that it takes two to make a child—which also means that, ideally, it takes two to raise one.

However, the reality of the fall—as well as the unpredictability of God's providence—means that families are never ideal. Sometimes that means women are left to raise their children alone.

How, then, do we apply the patterns outlined in this book to the single mother? Or is it even possible? What's the role of the church in the process? What about the extended family?

As usual, the Bible hasn't left us in the dark on the matter. God most assuredly has a heart for the widow and the orphan. "Father of the fatherless and protector of widows is God in his holy habitation" (Ps. 68:5; see also Lev. 19:10; Deut. 14:29; 16:11; 24:19–21; 26:12–13). And we would do well to apply this compassion of God to our own response in helping single mothers in this area.

IN THE OLD TESTAMENT

The Old Testament is replete with examples of God's care for widows and orphans—and of judgment upon those who oppress them. In fact, one of his principle grievances against his people Israel—resulting eventually in their captivity—was that "they do not bring justice to the fatherless, and the widow's cause does not come to them" (Isa. 1:23).

And yet at times Israel was a shining example of benevolence to widows and orphans. We see this in many ways, but the two principle means were the gleaning laws (Lev. 19:10) and levirate marriage (Gen. 38:6–26; Deut. 25:5–10). In both provisions we see a clear picture of the difficulty inherent in raising children alone and the importance of the community of faith in lightening the load.

Much could be said about the Old Testament practice of taking care of widows, orphans, foreigners, Levites, and the poor. However, the question we must ponder is, how does this translate in the New Covenant? How do we help single mothers today? Specifically, how do we help them exercise their role as family shepherds?

The New Testament gives us the framework.

IN THE NEW TESTAMENT

The clearest expression of the New Testament approach to ministry toward widows (and, by extension, to orphans) is found in Paul's first epistle to Timothy:

> Honor widows who are truly widows. But if a widow has children or grandchildren, let them first learn to show godliness to their own household and to make some return to their parents, for this is pleasing in the sight of God. She who is truly a widow, left all alone, has set her hope on God and continues in supplications and prayers night and day, but she who is self-indulgent is dead even while she lives. Command these things as well, so that they may be without reproach. But if anyone does not provide for his relatives, and especially for members of his household, he has denied the faith and is worse than an unbeliever. (1 Tim. 5:3–8)

There's much more in these verses than we can unpack here, and the issues addressed go far beyond this book's purpose. Nevertheless, we see a pattern that gives us a framework for thinking through our approach to family shepherding in the context of a single-parent home.

The text outlines three main levels of responsibility. The first is that of the nuclear family. The second that of the extended family. The third and final level of responsibility is that of the faith community. These levels of responsibility don't change simply because a father is absent from the home. Therefore, single mothers need to keep them in mind.

LEVEL ONE RESPONSIBILITY: THE NUCLEAR FAMILY

First, there's a man's responsibility to his immediate family. Paul's words in 1 Timothy 5:8 represent the strongest rebuke possible. What could the apostle possibly say to a man that would be stronger than this: "You have denied the faith and are worse than an unbeliever"? Moreover, the context here is caring for widows. Thus, Paul is leveling this charge not against a man who refuses to take care of his wife and children, but against a man who fails to care for his widowed mother! How much worse is it when a man finds himself neglecting the former?

We clearly see that the biblical lines of accountability and responsibility for family welfare begin with the nuclear family. This fact doesn't change when a woman finds herself raising children alone. Difficult though it may be, a single mother's first resource for the discipleship of her children is staring back at her in the mirror.

Regardless of the extenuating circumstances, a single mother must recognize that the primary responsibility for shepherding her family lies with her. A single-parent home is no less a family and has no less responsibility for raising children in the discipline and instruction of the Lord (Eph. 6:4) than do other families. This means a single mother must first look to the resources she has at hand, and she must make every effort to carry out the tasks expounded upon in this book.

LEVEL TWO RESPONSIBILITY: EXTENDED FAMILY

Second, adult children and the extended family are to care for the widow or single mother. "But if a widow has children or grandchildren, let them first learn to show godliness to their own household and to make some return to their parents, for this is pleasing in the sight of God" (1 Tim. 5:4). This means brothers, uncles, and even older sons can and should be a resource for a single mother whenever possible.

This doesn't mean she should call on extended family to bear the day-to-day burden of shepherding her family. That would violate the first principle of self-government, or one's duty to see to the needs of one's own household. However, there are times when a single mother needs help with a growing son, for example, when it would be very appropriate to call on a male relative for advice or intervention.

LEVEL THREE RESPONSIBILITY: THE CHURCH

Finally, there's the responsibility of the church family. Many people are surprised to discover that Paul puts the church last, not first, in the line of defense for the widow/single mother. This is due in part to unbiblical patterns that more closely resemble the work of social welfare agencies than the New Testament church. Consequently, many Christians would be offended to have a pastor advise a single mother to call on her extended family for help before coming to the church for it. However, that's precisely the biblical thing to do! The church is the last line of defense.

And there's good reason for this.

The church has limited jurisdiction. God designed the world with three distinct institutions—the family, the church, and the civil government—each with specific jurisdictions. The church can no more tell a family how to run its affairs than it can tell the state how to run theirs. Certainly, the church has a responsibility to teach, admonish, warn, and guide. However, it may not govern the other jurisdictions.

Children are commanded to obey their parents, not the church (Eph. 6:1; Col. 3:20).[1] As a result, the church is limited in what it can and cannot do for families. The day-to-day discipleship of children is outside those limits.

The church has limited access. In addition to limited jurisdiction, the church has limited access when it comes to shepherding families. The issues outlined in this book are of a day-to-day nature. This is something that requires a kind of ongoing access, which would be impossible (and quite inappropriate) for the church. What can the church be expected to accomplish on a weekly basis compared to the daily pursuits outlined in this book?

Moreover, the shepherding approach outlined in this book *assumes* the church's proper role—that is, what the church does in addition to (not as a substitute for) the family approach to shepherding.

The church has limited resources. Though there are myriad megachurches in our culture, the average Christian church has less than one hundred members. And even a ten-thousand-member megachurch has a limit when it comes to resources. There are only so many people, so much time, and so much money to go around. Logistically speaking, it would be impossible for any church to step in and meet all the needs of all the families lacking fathers.

This isn't to say the church has no obligation to help; it does. Nevertheless, that help has limits. Those limits include resources, access, and—most importantly—jurisdiction. Therefore, whatever the church does to help single parent homes, it must be governed by Scripture. And what you expect from your church must be governed by God's Word as well.

There are, however, several things the church can and must do to assist single mothers as they strive to do the work of shepherding a family alone.

PASTORAL CARE

The entire premise of 1 Timothy 5 is based on the assumption that the pastor/elder has a duty to lead and instruct the church in matters concerning widows and single mothers. In verse 7, Paul tells Timothy to "command these things." Moreover, the tenor of the passage indicates pastoral authority and responsibility in the matter. The apostle is giving young Timothy clear instructions that he's to follow in his duties as pastor, which in turn translates to all those who hold the office subsequently.

Pastors serve as a resource to teach, counsel, encourage, and admonish single mothers in the matter of shepherding their families. They have neither the jurisdiction nor the influence necessary to replace a father in the home. However, they have both a duty and a tremendous opportunity to provide clear biblical instruction and encourage application. This can mean taking young men aside for one-on-one instruction, providing opportunities for single mothers to receive the same instruction given to other family shepherds in a setting more suitable for them, and instructing extended family members as to their biblical responsibility to the single mother (1 Tim. 5:4, 7).

DIACONAL MINISTRY

The subsequent paragraph in 1 Timothy 5 (vv. 9–16) outlines a detailed diaconal ministry. Whereas elders are assigned the task of teaching, deacons have the responsibility of implementation (see also Acts 6). This may take the form of visitation, benevolence, or oversight. I've seen this type of ministry take the form of changing the oil in a single mother's car, performing household maintenance, taking boys to ballgames, and watching children while mom gets some needed rest.[2] However, there are myriad ways in which a diaconal ministry can be leveraged to offer ongoing, tangible, meaningful ministry to single mothers—much like Job, who "caused the widow's heart to sing for joy" (Job 29:13).

TITUS 2

The second chapter in Titus outlines the biblical and theological foundations for a three-pronged approach to churchwide family shepherding ministry. This is never more crucial than when it comes to single mothers. Godly, older men and women in the church, plus godly, manly elders, as well as biblically functioning homes all serve together as a tremendous environment and support for the fatherless. Those who grow up without fathers need to see families functioning around them who do have strong male leadership. This serves to show them (1) the biblical model in action, and (2) the fact that problems and difficulties are not unique to their particular situation.

The church was never intended to be a substitute for healthy family life. However, it is most assuredly designed to be an aid and buttress. Single mothers have a tremendous responsibility, and that responsibility cannot and must not be pawned off on others.

A single mother is as much a family shepherd as anyone. She must see her extended family and her church as resources to strengthen her hand. Thus, while she may in a real sense be by herself in this duty, she doesn't truly stand alone. "He executes justice for the fatherless and the widow, and loves the sojourner, giving him food and clothing" (Deut. 10:18).

APPENDIX ONE

TOOLS, FOLLOW-UP, AND ACCOUNTABILITY

The approach to shepherding described in this book is new to most men. Therefore, I am committed to providing tools and support for family shepherds.

HANDS-ON TOOLS

Our church provides a number of hands-on tools ranging from books and booklets to CDs and DVDs. However, the key tools are the prayer gram, worship guide, and monthly men's meeting.

PRAYER GRAM

The prayer gram is a weekly e-mail sent to every family in our church. It is divided into four key sections: *Pray for One Another* (five member families each week), *Pray for Kings and Those in Authority* (one local, one state, and one national leader each week), *Pray for the Gospel to Spread among All Peoples* (a different unreached or underreached people group each week), and *Pray for Those Who Feed, Lead, and Care for the Flock* (our elders and deacons).

The prayer gram is designed to guide family shepherds as they lead their families in prayer and teach their families to pray. The weekly e-mail helps eliminate monotony by updating the people and purposes for which we pray, while also keeping our church on the same page in our ongoing prayer. For an example of our prayer gram, see Appendix 2.

WORSHIP GUIDE

Our weekly worship guide serves as an order of worship and a corporate expression of our weekly prayer gram. Each week in our service we open with a pastoral prayer wherein we pray through the weekly prayer gram. This serves to unite our hearts in prayer, but it is also a model for family shepherds as the elders do corporately what they are being called to do privately in their homes. The worship guide also has our hymn of the month, which family shepherds can use along with the prayer gram for daily family worship.

MONTHLY MEN'S MEETING

Our monthly men's meeting is where we walk family shepherds through the outline of this book. Our year is broken up into quarters. The first quarter is devoted to *family evangelism/discipleship*, the second quarter to *marriage enrichment*, the third quarter to *child training*, and the fourth quarter to *lifestyle evaluation*. Thus, we spend three months concentrating on each of the categories covered in this book.

Each month we have a book of the month (though sometimes we concentrate on one book for an entire quarter), which our men read. Group discussion, teaching time, small-group prayer/feedback, and fellowship focus on the same topic.

ONE-ON-ONE MINISTRY

In addition to our weekly and monthly tools, we offer family shepherds one-on-one discipleship, accountability, and encouragement through our pastoral care ministry.

FELLOWSHIP MEAL

Each week we have a fellowship meal after church. In addition to being an invaluable opportunity to share life together, reflect on the service, and encourage one another, this is an informal time that allows family shepherds to approach mature men in the church (including the elders) with questions they may have concerning their roles, goals, and duties in the home.

HOSPITALITY

We encourage members of our church to practice biblical hospitality by inviting someone from the church and someone from their neighborhood over for food, fellowship, and family worship. That is the culture we have attempted to foster.

This is a tremendous outreach and in-reach tool. The inexperienced family shepherd has an opportunity to visit the home of another member and see how they do hospitality (lifestyle evaluation), interact with their family (marriage enrichment/child training), and conduct family worship (family evangelism/discipleship).

MONTHLY SHEPHERDING CALL

Our families are divided into districts with each elder responsible for a portion of the membership. Our goal is to contact each family shepherd at least once each month by phone and/or in person to pray, assess spiritual needs, answer questions, and fellowship with and encourage one another. It is also a perfect time for the elders to make sure each man is "picking up what we're putting down" in the monthly men's meeting.

Family shepherds have a chance to ask clarifying questions, make application to specific issues in their home, and even offer additional insights. This turns the monthly men's meeting into more of a dialogue than the normal monologue that has come to characterize much of modern discipleship. This type of interaction allows for the kind of honesty and transparency that rarely occurs in large or small group settings.

ANNUAL HOME VISIT

Finally, we attempt to visit each home for an annual elder home visit. This is an official visit designed to assess the spiritual condition of the family as well as give them opportunity to ask questions and address any pertinent issues.

This comprehensive approach may seem daunting. However, we have discovered that this would have been the norm in pastoral ministry in ages past (see Richard Baxter's book, *The Reformed Pastor*, for example), and this kind of active approach to shepherding the flock actually heads off many of the issues that become major problems if left unaddressed.

APPENDIX TWO

SAMPLE PRAYER GRAM

This is a sample prayer gram (with names altered to protect the identity of our members).

PRAY FOR ONE ANOTHER (JAMES 5:16)

Adams Family	Baker Family	Cooper Family	Davis Family	Evans Family
John	Jim & Tammy	Mark & Fran	Earnie & Beverly	Mike & Jenny
		John	Ashlee	David
		Allison	Anthony	Emma
		Nathan	Austin	Charis
		Megan	Audree	Abigail
			Asa	Providence
			Baby on the Way	

PRAY FOR KINGS AND THOSE IN AUTHORITY (1 TIM. 2:2)

Local	State	Nation
Mayor Annise Parker	Governor Rick Perry	President Barack Obama

PRAY FOR THE GOSPEL TO SPREAD AMONG ALL PEOPLES (MATT. 9:37–38)

BRAHMIN OF NEPAL

Brahmin is a Hindu Indian caste. The English word "Brahmin" is an anglicized form of the Sanskrit word "Brahmana." "Brahman" refers to the "Supreme Self" in Hinduism or the first of the gods. "Brahmin" refers to an individual.

In 1931 (the last Indian census to record caste), Brahmins accounted for 4.32 percent of the total Indian population. Due to the diversity in religious and cultural traditions and practices, and the Vedic schools to which they belong, Brahmins are further divided into various subcastes.

Brahmins perform Vedic rituals, but only a subset of Brahmins are involved in priestly duties, including teaching and preaching. They have excelled as educators, lawmakers, scholars, doctors, warriors, writers, poets, landowners and politicians. Many famous Indians are Brahmins.

The history of the Brahmins is associated with the Vedic religion of early Hinduism, usually referred to as Sanatana Dharma. The Vedas are the primary source for Brahmin practices. Over time, Brahmins became a powerful and influential group in India, and many discriminated against lower castes. However, in modern India some Brahmins claim reverse discrimination.

Where Are They Located?

Brahmins are located throughout India but are mainly in the northern states such as Uttar Pradesh and Andhra Pradesh. Small concentrations are in the southern Indian states of Tamil Nadu, Karnataka, and Kerala.

What Are Their Lives Like?

Brahmins are enjoined to offer prayers three times a day as prescribed in the Vedas.

Most Brahmins today are vegetarians or lacto-vegetarians. Nonvegetarian Brahmins are mainly those in cooler mountain areas like Kashmir, Himachal Pradesh, and Nepal. In some coastal areas like Bengal, Brahmins are fish eaters.

What Are Their Beliefs?

Brahmins can be identified by the three Hindu paths of Devotion, Knowledge, and Yoga, which they espouse in order for a person to achieve "god realization," the ultimate aim of the Hindu religion. All Brahmin teachings and writings relate to one of these paths. One is free to choose the path depending upon a person's inclination. Brahmins are Vedic priests, and they have three compulsory occupations—studying the Vedas, worshiping deities, and charitable giving.

Brahmin Christians: less than 2 percent
Scriptures in Nepali: complete Bible
Churches: localized church planting within past two years

PRAY FOR THOSE WHO FEED, LEAD, AND CARE FOR THE FLOCK (COL. 4:3; 2 THESS. 3:1)

Elders	Deacons
Pastor Voddie	Erin
Pastor Dale	Steven
Pastor Stephen	Marshall
	Mark
	Eddy
	Stuart
	Jeff
	Pete
	Rob

OUR SERMON TEXT FOR THIS WEEK IS ROMANS 12:14–18

Bless those who persecute you; bless and do not curse them. Rejoice with those who rejoice, weep with those who weep. Live in harmony with one another. Do not be haughty, but associate with the lowly. Never be wise in your own sight. Repay no one evil for evil, but give thought to do what is honorable in the sight of all. If possible, so far as it depends on you, live peaceably with all.

NOTES

CHAPTER 1: THE BIBLE AND THE FAMILY'S ROLE IN DISCIPLESHIP

1. Charles Hodge, *Systematic Theology*, vol. 3 (New York: C. Scribner, 1871), 706.

2. Charles H. Spurgeon, *Morning and Evening: Daily Reading*, reading for July 11, evening (numerous editions available).

3. Alfred Edersheim, *Sketches of Jewish Social Life in the Days of Christ* (Bellingham, WA: Logos Research Systems, 2003), 96.

4. Jim Hamilton, "That the Coming Generation Might Praise the Lord," *The Journal of Family Ministry* 1, no. 1 (Fall 2010): 10.

5. Ibid.

6. See Köstenberger, *God, Marriage and Family*. The relevant chapter can be accessed at Crosswalk. com, "Connecting Church and Family, Part 3," http://www.crosswalk.com/pastors/11634402/page0/. See also Sam Waldron, "The Relation of Church and Family," Reformed Baptist Fellowship, September 9, 2009, http://reformedbaptistfellowship.wordpress.com/2009/09/09/the-relation-of-church-and-family/. Note that Waldron has issued an open letter wherein he retracts some of his statements: Waldron, "An Open Letter with regard to My Blog on the Family-Integrated Church Movement," Reformed Baptist Fellowship, January 6, 2010, http://reformedbaptistfellowship.wordpress.com/2010/01/06/an-open-letter-with-regard-to-my-blog-on-the-family-integrated-church-movement/.

7. Edersheim, *Sketches of Jewish Social Life*, 159.

8. Robert L. Plummer, "Bring Them Up in the Discipline and Instruction of the Lord," *The Journal of Family Ministry* 1, no. 1 (Fall 2010): 20.

9. Andrew Stirrup, "From Whom Every Family in Heaven and on Earth Is Named," *The Journal of Family Ministry* 1, no. 1 (Fall 2010): 33. Emphasis added.

CHAPTER 2: A THREE-PRONGED APPROACH TO BIBLICAL DISCIPLESHIP

1. The order I chose to present the legs on the stool does not denote their rank or importance. The first leg could just as easily be the third.

2. Charles Duke Yonge, ed., *The Works of Philo* (Peabody, MA: Hendrickson, 1996), 2.226.

3. D. Edmond Hiebert, *Titus*, vol. 11, *Expositor's Bible Commentary*, ed. Frank E. Gaebelein (Grand Rapids, MI: Zondervan, 1978), 435.

4. John Calvin, *Calvin's Commentaries (Complete)*, trans. John King (Edinburgh: Calvin Translation Society, 1847), at Titus 2:2.

5. Ibid., at Titus 1:11.

6. Richard Baxter, *The Reformed Pastor*, in *Select Works of Richard Baxter* (Altamonte Springs, FL: OakTree Software, 2006), ii.

CHAPTER 4: HERALDING THE GOSPEL AT HOME

1. Don Carson, "The Gospel of Jesus Christ (1 Corinthians 15:1–19)," *The Spurgeon Fellowship Journal* (Spring 2008), reprinted with permission from The Gospel Coalition, http://www.thegospelcoalition.org/articles.php?a=81n.

2. Tim Keller, "The Centrality of the Gospel," Liberti, March 24, 2011, http://www.libertichurchcentercity.org/The-Centrality-Of-The-Gospel-By-Tim-Keller.

3. Carson, "The Gospel of Jesus Christ (1 Corinthians 15:1–19)."

4. John Hendryx, "What Is the Gospel?" Monergism, 2009, http://www.monergism.com/thethreshold/articles/onsite/qna/whatisgospel.html.

5. Michael Horton, *The Gospel-Driven Life: Being Good News People in a Bad News World* (Grand Rapids, MI: Baker, 2009), 20.

6. Andreas Köstenberger, "The Gospel for All Nations," in *Faith Comes by Hearing: A Response to Inclusivism*, ed. Christopher W. Morgan and Robert A. Peterson (Downers Grove, IL: InterVarsity, 2008), 218. Also in Chris Blackstone, "What Is the Gospel? Five Observations," *Intersected* (blog), February 12, 2010, http://intersected.org/category/faith/gospel/page/2/. See also Andreas Köstenberger and Peter O'Brien, *Salvation to the Ends of the Earth* (Downers Grove, IL: InterVarsity Press, 2001), 227–32.

7. Hendryx, "What Is the Gospel?"

CHAPTER 5: CATECHISM AND CHRISTIAN EDUCATION

1. Jonathan Edwards, letter to James Robe, May 23, 1749, as quoted by Sereno E. Dwight in *Life of President Edwards,* ed. Edward Hickman, in *Works of President Edwards: With a Memoir of His Life in Ten Volumes* (New York: S. Converse, 1829), 1:282.

2. Zacharias Ursinus, "What Is Catechism?" *Commentary on the Heidelberg Catechism,* trans. G. W. Williard (Phillipsburg, NJ: P&R; repr., 1992; orig., 1852), n.p.

3. Richard Baxter, *The Reformed Pastor,* ed. William Brown (London: Religious Tract Society, 1829), 91.

4. Ibid., 93.

5. B. B. Warfield, "Is the Shorter Catechism Worthwhile?" The Westminster Presbyterian, http://www.westminsterconfession.org/confessional-standards/is-the-shorter-catechism-worth while.php.

CHAPTER 6: FAMILY WORSHIP

1. See Voddie Baucham, *Family Driven Faith* (Wheaton, IL: Crossway, 2007) and *What He Must Be: If He Wants to Marry My Daughter* (Wheaton, IL: Crossway, 2009).

2. George Whitefield, "The Great Duty of Family Religion," in *Fifteen Sermons Preached on Various Important Subjects by George Whitefield* (Glasgow, Scotland: Paisley, 1794), 255.

3. Ibid., 256.

4. Ibid., 257.

5. Ibid.

6. James W. Alexander, *Thoughts on Family Worship* (Philadelphia: Presbyterian Board of Education, 1847).

7. David Wegener, "A Father's Role in Family Worship: A Review of James W. Alexander's Classic Work *Thoughts on Family Worship," Journal of the Council on Biblical Manhood and Womanhood* (vol. 3, no. 4), http://www.cbmw.org/Journal/Vol-3-No-4/A-Father-s-Role-in-Family-Worship.

8. Whitefield, "The Great Duty of Family Religion," 258–59.

9. Loraine Boettner, *The Reformed Doctrine of Predestination* (Grand Rapids, MI: Eerdmans, 1932). This paragraph is in section 3, "Objections Commonly Urged against the Reformed Doctrine of Predestination," as the opening lines of chapter 18, "That It Discourages All Motives to Exertion," Full-Proof Ministries, http://www.full-proof.org/wp-content/uploads/2010/04/Boettner-Reformed-Doctrine-of-Predestination.pdf.

10. Whitefield, "The Great Duty of Family Religion," 259–60.

CHAPTER 7: THE PURPOSE OF MARRIAGE

1. John H. Sailhamer, *Genesis,* vol. 2, *Expositors Bible Commentary,* ed. Frank E. Gabelein (Grand Rapids, MI: Zondervan, 1990), 38.

2. "The water" could be a reference to baptism, or the washing of the bride before the marriage ceremony. Also, "the word" could be a reference to the words spoken by the baptismal candidate, or the officiate. See, for example, A. Skevington Wood, *Ephesians,* vol. 11, *Expositors Bible Commentary,* ed. Frank E. Gabelein (Grand Rapids, MI: Zondervan, 1978), 76–77.

CHAPTER 8: THE PRIMACY OF MARRIAGE

1. "Last Name Meanings—Surnames," Family History UK, http://www.familyhistory.uk.com/ index.php?option=com_content&task=view&id=18&Itemid=29.

CHAPTER 9: MALE HEADSHIP IN THE HOME

1. "Evangelical feminism" is the term used to identify egalitarians in the church as opposed to feminists outside the church. Evangelical feminists differ in that they acknowledge the Bible as authoritative, although they have come to different conclusions on the matter of male headship.

2. Daniel Doriani, "The Historical Novelty of Egalitarian Interpretations of Ephesians 5:21–22," *Biblical Foundations for Manhood and Womanhood,* ed. Wayne Grudem (Wheaton, IL: Crossway, 2002), 204.

3. While there are a number of other objections, and many ways to list and classify them, I am relying on Daniel Doriani's order because I believe he captures the essence of the main objections and orders them in a way that is logical and accessible. I did, however, omit Doriani's first listed objection (that the passage is a confusing mystery because of v. 21) since it is actually a subset of the final argument.

Notes

4. See, for example, Thomas R. Schreiner, "Head Coverings, Prophecies, and the Trinity: 1 Corinthians 11:2–16," *Recovering Biblical Manhood and Womanhood: A Response to Evangelical Feminism*, eds. John Piper and Wayne Grudem (Wheaton, IL: Crossway, 1991).

5. Aida Spencer, *Beyond the Curse* (Peabody, MA: Hendrickson, 1985), 35. Quoted in Doriani, "Historical Novelty," 206.

6. See my discussion in *Family Driven Faith: Doing What It Takes to Raise Sons and Daughters Who Walk with God* (Wheaton, IL: Crossway, 2004).

7. Andrea Dworkin, *Letters from a War Zone: Writings from 1976–1989* (New York: Lawrence Hill Books, 1993), 308.

8. Robin Morgan, http://www.robinmorgan.us/robin_morgan_bio.asp. These are not obscure women making noise at small rallies where no one is listening. This is the mainstream.

9. Robin Morgan, *Sisterhood Is Powerful* (New York: Vintage, 1970), 537.

10. Linda Gordon, "Functions of the Family," in *WOMEN: A Journal of Liberation* (Fall, 1969), n.p.

11. Raymond C. Ortlund Jr., "Male-Female Equality and Male Headship: Genesis 1–3," in *Recovering Biblical Manhood and Womanhood: A Response to Evangelical Feminism*, eds. John Piper and Wayne Grudem (Wheaton, IL: Crossway, 1991), 86.

12. See Robin Morgan, "Theory and Practice: Pornography and Rape" in *Going too Far: The Personal Chronicle of a Feminist* (New York: Random House, 1974); and Dworkin, *Letters from a War Zone*.

13. Suzette Haden Elgin, "A Feminist Is a What?" in *Women and Language*, vol. 18, no. 2 (1995): 46. Available at http://www.questia.com/PM.qst?a=o&d=5000390350.

14. Andrea Dworkin, *Our Blood: Prophecies and Discourses on Sexual Politics* (New York: Harper & Row, 1976), 20.

15. Ortlund, "Male-Female Equality and Male Headship," 65.

16. John Piper and Wayne Grudem, "An Overview of Central Concerns: Questions and Answers," in *Recovering Biblical Manhood and Womanhood: A Response to Evangelical Feminism* (Wheaton, IL: Crossway, 1991), 66–67.

CHAPTER 10: REMEMBERING THE FALL

1. Horatius Bonar, *How Shall I Go to God?—And Other Readings* (London: Religious Tract Society, 1883), 5.

2. James C. Robertson, *Sketches of Church History: From A.D. 33 to the Reformation* (London: Society for Promoting Christian Knowledge, 1912), 124.

3. Gregg R. Allison, *Historical Theology: An Introduction to Christian Doctrine* (Grand Rapids, MI: Zondervan, 2011), 345.

4. Ibid., 346.

5. Ibid., 347–48.

6. B. B. Warfield, "What Is Calvinism?" in *Selected Shorter Writings of Benjamin B. Warfield*, ed. John E. Meeter (Phillipsburg, NJ: P&R, 1970), 1:389; originally published in *The Presbyterian* (March 2, 1904), 6–7.

7. From A. A. Hodge, *Outlines of Theology* (New York: Robert Carter & Brothers, 1860), as summarized in "Pelagianism, Semi-Pelagianism, and Augustinianism," ed. Shane Rosenthal, at Monergism, http://www.monergism.com/thethreshold/articles/onsite/semi-pelagian.html.

8. Charles Hodge, *Systematic Theology*, vol. 2 (New York: C. Scribner, 1871), 106.

9. Michael Pearl, *To Train Up a Child* (Pleasantville, TN: No Greater Joy Ministries, 1994), 17. Emphasis added.

10. Ibid., 18.

11. Ibid.

12. Ibid., 21.

13. Ibid., 22.

14. Tedd Tripp, *Shepherding a Child's Heart* (Wapwallopen, PA: Shepherd Press, 1995), 4.

15. Ibid., xxi.

16. Robert Shaw, *The Reformed Faith: An Exposition of the Confession of Faith of the Westminster Assembly of Divines* (Glasgow: Blackie and Son, 1857; Altamonte Springs, FL: OakTree Software, 2001); chap. 6.

17. Tripp, *Shepherding a Child's Heart*, 164.

18. A few suggestions: Elyse Fitzpatrick, *Give Them Grace: Dazzling Your Kids with the Love of Jesus* (Wheaton, IL: Crossway, 2011); William P. Farley, *Gospel-Powered Parenting: How the Gospel Shapes and Transforms Parenting* (Phillipsburg, NJ: P&R, 2009); and *Gospel-Centred Family: Becoming*

the Parents God Wants You to Be by Tim Chester and Ed Moll (New Malden, Surrey, England: Good Book Company, 2009).

CHAPTER 11: FORMATIVE DISCIPLINE

1. Cotton Mather, *A Family Well-Ordered*, ed. Don Kistler (Morgan, PA: Soli Deo Gloria Publications, 2001), n.p.

2. Formative discipline differs from corrective discipline in that formative discipline is the instruction and training we build into the lives of our children, whereas corrective discipline is our response to their disobedience.

3. This is not to say that such errors did not exist, but the full-orbed versions with which we wrestle today were not as normative or prevalent then.

4. Mather also included a seventh principle that addresses infant baptism.

5. Mather, *A Family Well-Ordered*, 4.

6. John Wesley, "On Family Religion," in *Sermons on Several Occasions*, vol. 3 (New York: J & J Harper, 1831), 117.

7. Mather, *A Family Well-Ordered*, 10.

8. Wesley, "On Family Religion," 118.

9. Mather, *A Family Well-Ordered*, 13.

10. Ibid., 14.

11. Ibid., 14–15.

12. Ibid., 18.

13. Ibid., 19.

14. Cotton Mather, *Help for Distressed Parents*, ed. Don Kistler (Morgan, PA: Soli Deo Gloria, repr. ed., 2004), 10.

15. Mather, *A Family Well-Ordered*, 19.

16. Ibid., 20.

17. Ibid.

CHAPTER 12: CORRECTIVE DISCIPLINE

1. Jonathan Edwards, "Christian Cautions: or, The Necessity of Self-Examination" in *The Works of Jonathan Edwards* (New York: Daniel Appleton and Co., 1835), 1:183.

2. Kenelm F. McCormick, "Attitudes of Primary Care Physicians toward Corporal Punishment," *Journal of the American Medical Association*, 267 [23] (1992): 3161. Cited by Abraham A. Andero and Allen Stewart in "Issue of Corporal Punishment: Re-examined," *Journal of Instructional Psychology*, vol. 29, no. 2, (2002), http://www.questia.com/PM.qst?a=o&d=5000788637.

3. Paul D. Wegner, "Discipline in the Book of Proverbs: 'To Spank or Not to Spank?'" *Journal of the Evangelical Theological Society*, vol. 48, no. 4 (December 2005): 715–32, http://www.questia.com/PM.qst?a=o&d=5036781927.

4. Ibid., 726.

5. Though this is obviously tongue-in-cheek, many wonder when a child is "too old to spank." They want a magic number, an age beyond which spanking is off limits. I do not believe it is wise, or even possible, to determine such an age. First, every child is different. Children mature at different rates. Second, the Bible does not operate like a paint-by-numbers kit when it comes to discipline and correction. Parents will have to be wise and discerning and evaluate each child individually to determine when it is appropriate to stop spanking.

6. *New International Dictionary of Old Testament Theology and Exegesis*, ed. Wilhelm A. VanGemeren, vol. 3 (Grand Rapids, MI: Zondervan, 1997), 433.

7. Paul R. Gilchrist, "Yakah: Decide, Judge, Prove, Rebuke, Reprove, Correct," in *Theological Wordbook of the Old Testament*, ed. R. Laird Harris, vol. 1 (Chicago: Moody Press, 1980), 377.

8. Wegner, "Discipline in the Book of Proverbs," 726.

9. John Wesley, "On Family Religion," Sermon XCIX in *Sermons on Several Occasions*, vol. 3 (New York: J & J Harper, 1831), n.p.

10. Ibid., 117.

11. Randall J. Heskett, "Between Text & Sermon: Proverbs 23:13–14," in *Interpretation*, vol. 55, no. 2 (2001): 181, http://www.questia.com/PM.qst?a=o&d=5037676858.

12. Ibid.

Notes

CHAPTER 13: CHURCH MEMBERSHIP

1. Mark Dever, *A Display of God's Glory: Basics of Church Structure, Deacons, Elders, Congregationalism, and Church Membership* (Washington, DC: The Center for Church Reform, 2001), 45.

2. Ibid.

3. Ibid., 50.

4. The London Baptist Confession of 1689, chap. 26, sec. 5, Christian Classics Ethereal Library, http://www.ccel.org/creeds/bcf/bcfc26.htm#chapter26.

CHAPTER 14: OUR USE OF TIME

1. B. B. Warfield, "The Foundations of the Sabbath in the Word of God," address delivered at the Fourteenth International Lord's Day Congress in Oakland, California, July 27–August 1, 1915; published in *Sunday: The World's Rest Day* (Garden City, NY: Doubleday, 1916), 63–81, and in *The Free Presbyterian Magazine* (Glasgow, Scotland, 1918), 316–19, 335–54, 378–83. Available at The Highway, http://www.the-highway.com/Sabbath_Warfield.html.

2. Thomas Boston, "On the Fourth Commandment," *An Illustration of the Doctrines of the Christian Religion* (Edinburgh: John Reid, 1773), 2:568; Also published as "The Sanctification of the Sabbath," The Westminster Presbyterian, http://www.westminsterconfession.org/worship/the-sanctification-of-the-sabbath.php.

3. Boston, "On the Fourth Commandment," 2:565.

4. John Owen, *An Exposition of the Epistle to the Hebrews with Preliminary Exercitations*, second ed. (Edinburgh: J. Ritchie, 1812), 2:453.

CHAPTER 15: DUAL CITIZENSHIP

1. John mentions the world in John 1:9–10, 29; 3:16–17, 19; 4:42; 6:14, 33, 51; 7:4, 7; 8:12, 23, 26; 9:5, 32, 39; 10:36; 11:9, 27; 12:19, 25, 31, 46–47; 13:1; 14:17, 19, 22, 27, 30–31; 15:18–19; 16:8, 11, 20–21, 28, 33; 17:5–6, 9, 11, 13–16, 18, 21, 23–25; 18:20, 36–37; 21:25.

2. Kim Riddlebarger, "A Two Kingdoms Primer," *The Riddleblog* (blog), September 2, 2010, http://kimriddlebarger.squarespace.com/the-latest-post/2010/9/2/a-two-kingdoms-primer.html.

3. Ibid.

4. See also George Eldon Ladd, "What Is the Kingdom of God?" in *The Gospel of the Kingdom* (Grand Rapids, MI: Eerdmans, 1959), 13–23. Available at GospelPedlar, http://gospelpedlar.com/articles/Last%20Things/kogladd.html.

A SPECIAL CONCERN

1. Of course, regenerate children are obligated to "obey your leaders and submit to them" (Heb. 13:17). However, the church does not have the right to interfere with matters of the home. The pastor does not assign chores, inspect the cleanliness of rooms, make decisions about what's for dinner, etc. There are clear and necessary limits to church authority.

2. All these things must of course be done in such a way that propriety and purity are protected. For instance, deacons should not be alone with single women; their wives should be involved as much as possible. There can be regular rotation so no single deacon is spending too much time with a given family, etc.

Now Available from Voddie Baucham

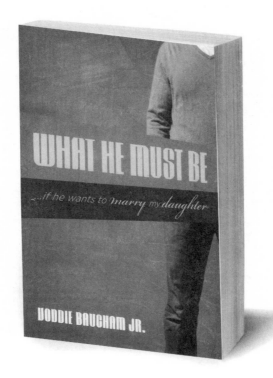

What will you say when that certain young man sits down in your living room, sweaty-palmed and tongue-tied, and asks your permission to marry your daughter? This compelling apologetic of biblical manhood outlines ten qualities parents should look for in a son-in-law.

Doing What It Takes to Raise Sons and Daughters Who Walk with God

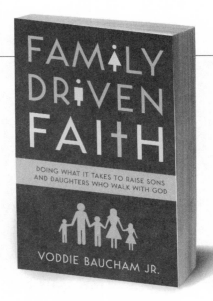

More teens are turning away from the faith than ever before: it is estimated that 75 to 88 percent of Christian teens walk away from Christianity by the end of their freshman year of college. Something must be done.

Family Driven Faith equips Christian parents with the tools they need to raise children biblically in a post-Christian, antifamily society. Voddie Baucham shows that God has not left us alone in raising godly children. In his Word he has given us timeless precepts and principles for multigenerational faithfulness.